Faith On First

Faith On First

Thoughts on God, Nature and Sacrifice Bunts

Charles Honey

FREEZE■FRAME
publishing

in cooperation with The Grand Rapids Press

FREEZE FRAME
publishing

Faith On First: Thoughts on God, Nature and Sacrifice Bunts © 2014 by Charles Honey.

Cover photograph © 2013 by T.J. Hamilton
Author photograph by T.J. Hamilton
Cover design by T.J. Hamilton, www.tjhamiltonphoto.com

Chapter illustrations © 2014 by Maxwell Honey

Grateful acknowledgement is made to The Grand Rapids Press for permission to reprint previously published material. Some column titles have been changed. These stories originally appeared in The Grand Rapids Press between 1995 and 2013, inclusive, except for *On Top of the World*, *Dreaming* and *Chasing Rainbows with Coltrane* which are from the author's blog, www.soulmailing.com, and *Just One More Thing* which was written specially for this book. All other pieces © 1995-2013 The Grand Rapids Press. All rights reserved.

Printed in the United States of America

Library of Congress Control Number: 2014933655

ISBN 978-0-9839868-6-7

To Keith and Betty Honey,
who taught me to respect all people,
to love writing, music and nature,
and to cheer for the Tigers

Contents

Acknowledgements

A long time ago, Chris Meehan and I sat across from each other in the office of the Williamston Enterprise, my hometown newspaper, and talked about how working at The Grand Rapids Press would be a pretty good gig someday.

Chris and I became friends and, in time, coworkers at The Grand Rapids Press. Chris was religion editor there before I was, winning an award in the 1980s for the best religion section in the country. He is one of the reasons I wrote this book.

Ed Golder is another. One day in the fall of 1994 Ed asked me if I would like to succeed him as religion editor, a mantle he'd inherited from Chris. I'm sure my eyes said, "Are you nuts?" But my mouth said yes and I never regretted it.

Chris and Ed are two of the many people I have to thank for this book. I am deeply grateful to have worked at The Press, which provided me the pulpit from which to write the columns and other writings collected here. From my boyhood onward I have loved to write, and The Press gave me the professional means to do so for nearly 25 years.

Over the years I have been privileged to work for many editors who nurtured and improved my writing. They included John Barnes, Ed Hoogterp, Sue Schroder, Julie Hoogland, Ben Beversluis, Ruth Butler, Paul Keep, Tanda Gmiter and the late Andy Angelo. I consider them all friends and teachers.

I am especially indebted to T.J. Hamilton, my longtime Press colleague, who took the beautiful photos and designed the jacket of this book; to Gary Schroder, my former assistant metro editor, who generously proofread and edited it; to Pat Shellenbarger, my longtime friend and former Press coworker, who wrote the lovely foreword; and to my son, Maxwell Honey, who provided the artwork fronting each chapter.

I am deeply indebted as well to Danny Gaydou, president, MLive Media Group,who graciously supported my work and authorized this project. And I owe a special thanks to former Editor Mike Lloyd, who hired me on in 1985 and always backed me fully as I grew into the job.

Reaching farther back, I am grateful to Harry Stapler, who hired me in high school to cover sports for the Williamston Enterprise and sent me to a journalism seminar at the University of Michigan. Without his encouragement I doubt I would have ended up in journalism.

Nor would I have believed as much in my abilities were it not for Winnifred Daignault, my high school English teacher who made my idea of becoming a writer seem not so crazy.

For learning the ropes of religion coverage I am deeply indebted to Debra L. Mason, president of the Religion Newswriters Association, and to my many colleagues at RNA who guided me through the strange and wonderful terrain of the God beat.

Also of great help in climbing that steep learning curve were scholars at Calvin, Aquinas and other colleges, who often saved me from committing foolishness in print.

For their strong spiritual support I thank my friends at Trinity United Methodist Church, and in particular the Rev. Gerald Pohly for baptizing this skeptical believer.

It has been such a gift to have readers whose praise has encouraged me and whose criticism has kept me honest. A special thanks to Fran Baron, who fashioned artfully poetic versions of my columns, and to the fascinating, faith-filled people who inspired these writings. It has been a privilege to tell their stories.

I could not have published this book without Laura Hughes, owner of Freeze Frame Publishing, who expertly showed me how to do it and patiently stayed with me until I finally did.

I would never have gotten to Grand Rapids, much less be blessed with two beautiful children, without the loving support and encouragement of my former wife, Wendy Honey.

Finally, I would be nowhere at all if it weren't for my precious family: my late parents, Keith and Betty; my wonderful sister and brother, Maureen and Mike; my dear children, Emily and Maxwell; and my cherished companion, Andrea Myers. They are the brightest lights of my life, whose love and delight make the world worth writing about.

Foreword

In the interest of full disclosure, I first should come clean: Charley Honey is a friend of mine. But, then, if you've read his columns, which have run in The Grand Rapids Press for many years, you, too, likely consider him a friend. That's the kind of writer he is — warm, engaging and affable while offering insight into the human condition and the eternal quest for a deeper meaning of life.

That's not to say Charley hasn't sometimes received poison-pen letters, emails and online comments. A reader once called him "Satan's puppet." Religion, after all, is very personal, and many believers are certain theirs is the one, true God. Charley is an egalitarian, treating each faith, or lack thereof, with respect.

He finds spirituality in the little things many of us, too busy to pause and bask in the joy of every day, take for granted. A cloudless summer sky, a snowbound winter's day, drinks with friends, and, of course, baseball all are sources of inspiration.

This is the real Charley Honey.

You might not know he is a guitarist, a song writer and namesake of a rock band, the Honeytones. He is an authority on the Beatles and can quote such obscure statistics as the batting averages of most members of the 1968 Detroit Tigers.

We met more than 30 years ago when Charley was editor of his hometown weekly, the Williamston Enterprise, and I recently had moved to town. We found our common interests extended beyond journalism. I can't begin to estimate how many miles we have run together, but it must be thousands.

Some years ago, Charley moved to Kentucky and I to Florida, but we kept in touch. One day in the mid-1980s, he called and told me he had been hired by The Grand Rapids Press.

"Really?" I said. "So have I."

For years, we sat across from each other in the newsroom. Often when I was unsure a particular piece I had written worked, I would ask Charley to read it. His suggestions always improved my stories.

Yes, it is journalism, but Charley practices a higher, literary form that makes his columns so compelling that they draw you in, whether you think you're interested or not. Always there is substance to what he writes. He is a reporter and a storyteller.

Charley does not preach but gives readers something to think about. He is drawn to the ordinary among us who have something extraordinary to say. Herein you'll find pieces that read like conversations between friends. A terminally ill man who spent 30 years in prison for a crime he didn't commit talks of faith and forgiveness. A father teaches his son to throw a curveball and to accept the curves life sometimes throws. A stranger on a beach looks out at his daughters splashing in the surf and remarks, "So beautiful."

That is the essence of what Charley writes. Beauty, spirituality and peace can be found in the Bible, the Quran, the Talmud and other religious texts. Take a moment to look around, he teaches us, and you'll find them everywhere.

Pat Shellenbarger, Opening Day, 2014

First Inning

Everyday Players

Storyteller puts grace in a comic light

So there's this guy sitting in the lobby of the Amway Grand Plaza Hotel, and he's showing me how to take the seeds out of a pepper with an imaginary Chinese cleaver. And then he says, "God is not terribly interested in spirituality. What he loves is matter. He's the biggest materialist in the universe. Because he owns it all, he made it all and he likes it a lot. He's got more stuff than anybody."

At that point, I know this is not a normal interview. Robert Farrar Capon is chattering with the utmost delight, delight in his dancing blue eyes, in his curling pipe, in the sunlight silhouetting his silver hair. And I say to myself, shut up and listen.

Because Capon is telling me the history of the world. Oh sure, he's a theologian, an Episcopal priest, a lecturer, an author and a cook. He's in town to talk to his editors at Eerdmans Publishing, which is soon coming out with his novel, "Between Noon and Three." And he preached at Grace Christian Reformed Church, where the Rev. Roger VanHarn has carried on a pen-pal friendship with him.

But what Capon really is, is a storyteller. The name of the story is grace, and it's darn funny. Forget the Episcopal priest; this New York-bred guy is as Jewish as Mel Brooks.

Let's start with the part where God created the world.

One afternoon God tells the son and Holy Spirit he's been thinking about things he could make: ducks, wine, mountains, girl's knees. The son takes the Holy Spirit aside and says, "Listen, he seems to be crazy about this. Why don't we mix him up a batch?"

So they do, and spend the rest of eternity having a ball. "There is a creation because there was a divine bash that created it," Capon says with a twinkle.

So then you get minerals, vegetables, animals, people, sex and romance, the Arc de Triomphe, yatta yatta yatta. Problem is, "We've managed to screw it up royally."

That would be Adam and Eve, back in Chapter 3. So God says to Abraham, "Your children are going to be the key to my plan for fixing this mess. Abraham says, 'You noticed I don't have children?' "

It's like a football game. God the father plays the first half. At halftime, he sends in Jesus, the divine quarterback. At the end of the third quarter, the father sends Jesus to the showers and sends in the Holy Spirit to finish the game. And guess what? Everybody wins.

"How does Jesus save the world?" Capon's really rolling now. "By making up a self-improvement course and saying, 'If you get this right, you can come home?' No. He says, 'I, if I be lifted up, will draw all to me.'

"God is interested in a universal salvation, in getting the whole show fixed, not setting up a club in the sky. . . . If he wants everybody, he's gotta pick a ticket that everybody has. There's only one: We all end up dead.

"The only thing you have to be to get raised from the dead is dead. Everybody rises, the just and the unjust, because Jesus rises."

This is where grace comes in, see. Grace is unqualified acceptance, the love that will not let you go no matter what you do. "You may despise the acceptance forever," Capon allows, "in which case you're in hell. But even those in hell are accepted."

Wait. Once in hell, can you get back out? Good question, Capon says, but adds, "In Jesus, they're already back out, because he's redeemed them. It's just that they don't believe it.

"Everybody will end up saved. What they do with it is up to them."

In other words, there's this great party going on, and everybody's invited. Buddhists, Baptists, atheists. Show up late at the vineyard, you still get a full day's wage. So drop dead to all your nonsense and enjoy it. And remember: Jesus is God incarnate, not an Amway salesman.

"You don't have to find him," Capon says, eyes still dancing. "He's done a number on you and everybody else that you don't have to do, because the job is done. He only asks you, 'Would you please shut up and trust me?' "

Oh, and one other thing. Forgive.

"Faith, the real act of trust, is the extension to everyone in your life of the forgiveness that has been extended to us. That's how we join the party."

And the moral of the story would be . . .?

"Thank him," Capon says, puffing on his pipe with delight. "Smile a lot. Laugh about the fact that it was that easy."

I love a great storyteller.

Sept. 28, 1996

'The whole thing is a miracle'

If you want to learn something about the power of faith, education and compassion, meet Clement Chiwaya. His radiant smile will warm your spirit. His generous heart will touch yours.

Then he will tell you about a village in Malawi that needs a well, and chances are you will help him dig it.

That is why this remarkable man, who showed up in Grand Rapids six years ago with nothing but $500 and a dream, returned Thursday to Aquinas College as a member of parliament.

Make that an MP who cannot walk — Chiwaya was stricken with polio as a child — and Malawi's first minister of social development and persons with disabilities.

Even before he was elected in May and appointed to the Cabinet-level post, Chiwaya had brought fresh water, desperately needed food and new schools to his impoverished African homeland — all with West Michigan's help.

This week, he came back to thank those who helped him become a force for change in Malawi.

"I regard America as my second home," Chiwaya said, midway through a weeklong visit. "I can't find a way to thank the people of West Michigan for what they've done for me."

That includes area businesses and foundations, Catholic Diocese officials and Aquinas faculty who befriended him on his way to graduation two years ago.

"You're the ones who have made me what I am today," Chiwaya, 33, told about 60 friends and supporters at Aquinas' Wege Center.

Most of those in the room would disagree. They will say it is Chiwaya's irresistible kindness and commitment that have drawn them to his side.

"The minute you meet him, you just know he's going to do important things in the world," said Lori Knapp, of Rockford, president of the Warm Hearts Foundation.

Working with Chiwaya, her charity funded two wells and a school in a remote mountain village.

Robert Woodrick contributed to Chiwaya's campaign and helped fund his development projects. The D&W Food Centers chairman recalled telling him, "Clement, you're the type of individual Africa needs in the government, because you're so committed to helping people.

"Wouldn't it be great if he's president?" Woodrick asked Thursday. "From this point on, that would not surprise me."

It wouldn't surprise me either, given how much Chiwaya has overcome and accomplished.

He grew up in a dirt-poor village, dragging his crippled legs to school in a country that disdains disabled people. He was taken in by a Catholic missionary when his Muslim mother could no longer care for him. He came to West Michigan with his hopes set on college before he'd even been accepted by one.

Here he was befriended by James Rademaker of the Catholic Diocese, who invited Chiwaya into his home and later set up a Malawi development fund. Rademaker worked closely with Aquinas officials who waived the normal red tape so Chiwaya could enroll in the school's Community Leadership program.

He took the lessons to heart. Chiwaya returned to his home village and introduced sustainable farming techniques, planted trees and built his mother a better home.

When asked to run for parliament, he readily accepted the challenge. He drove from village to village in a rebuilt 1990 Toyota, which Aquinas students had paid to have shipped from Japan. He, his wife and year-old baby stayed in a house with no electricity or windows, getting by largely on donations from West Michigan.

He won the election by a 2-to-1 margin, and now represents some 80 villages from his office in the capital city of Lilongwe. His family lives in a four-bedroom home in an upscale neighborhood, and a chauffeur drives him to appointments.

"The most amazing thing is that I became who I am because I came to America," he marveled, his warm eyes shining. "The whole thing is a miracle."

He's wasted no time tackling his priorities: poverty, the scourge of AIDS, discrimination against the disabled. He's ordered about 200 wheelchairs and crutches to give to hospitals.

"My big dream is to see the people of my country improve their livelihoods and living standards," he said. "I'll be happy when I see that."

The people of West Michigan will continue to help him realize that dream. It's not because of our generosity. It's because Clement has graced us with his.

Oct. 8, 2004

After 28 years, 'It's so great to be free'

I have had the privilege of meeting a man convicted of trying to kill someone

His name is Maurice Carter. He has gentle eyes, a warm hug and a soft smile that glows with gratitude.

In this thin, ailing man, I saw a presence of grace that I have not witnessed in a very long time.

"I know this God is for real," Carter said quietly, sitting in the lobby of an area nursing home. "He's just answered my prayers. That's what keeps me going."

It had been almost a month since Maurice Carter walked out of prison after 28 years behind bars. He went in at age 32, convicted in 1976 of assault with the intent to murder a Benton Harbor police officer. He came out at age 60 and suffering from hepatitis C, his life sentence commuted by Gov. Jennifer Granholm.

Granholm and the state Parole Board released Carter due to his declining health. He may need a liver transplant to survive.

That did not clear Carter's name from a crime he and many supporters say he did not commit. Based on the information I have seen, I believe they're almost certainly right.

But it wasn't the details of his case that drew me to Carter. It was his lack of bitterness after losing the prime of his life to prison. In him, I saw the power of faith to transform and transcend.

"God put me in there for a reason," Carter said of his imprisonment. "There was a reason I had to wait so long. I accept it now."

We were with Pat Shellenbarger, a Press reporter whose investigative articles drew attention to Carter's plight, and Ed Golder, a Press editorial writer who advocated his release.

Carter was staying in an assisted-living facility while being treated for a staph infection and awaiting evaluation for a possible liver transplant. As other patients were wheeled down the hall, Carter expressed a Rip Van Winkle-like wonder at how much had changed since he went behind bars.

"Things are so fast," he marveled. "They didn't have VCRs when I was out. The Internet, cell phones ..."

He calls his mother in Gary, Ind., regularly now but is restricted from visiting her for six months. For now, he finds comfort in the family of Doug Tjapkes of Spring Lake, who worked long and hard for his release.

Carter came to Tjapkes' congregation, Ferrysburg Community Church, after his release to express gratitude for church members' support and letters on his behalf. He and Tjapkes embraced to a standing ovation, and Carter nodded to a favorite hymn, "His Eye is on the Sparrow."

He figures God's eye was on him in prison. But it took Tjapkes to convince him of that.

After his conviction, he said, "I was really frustrated and bitter and angry. Didn't trust anybody. Sort of lost my faith."

A prison counselor began to change that, turning Carter back toward his better self and the Lord he had worshipped as a child. But it was when Tjapkes began visiting about 10 years ago that he really turned around.

"He'd say, 'Maurice, it's in God's hands.' I said, 'Give me a couple (Bible) verses and I'll read 'em.'"

Through prayer and a Bible study group, his faith revived. "It seemed like every time I asked God to help me, he came through." That's when he realized God had better things in mind than the life he'd been living, even before prison.

"I know what he put me on this earth for now. He wants me to help others. That's what life is all about — being around good people and doing God's work."

He plans to do so through the group Innocent!, which Tjapkes established, by helping wrongly convicted inmates.

But until his health improves, Carter is just drinking in the beauty of being alive. He rhapsodized about eating steak and salmon from Doug and Marcia Tjapkes' grill, and about how he felt when he got out of prison.

"It was just a great day," he said, hands open. "I felt the breeze; I saw the sun. It's so great to be free."

We walked out back of the nursing home, where fish jumped in the Grand River and a light breeze blew through soft sunshine. Standing next to Maurice Carter, I was grateful to be alive — and free.

Aug. 21, 2004

Following is an entry from Matt Tjapkes, Doug's son, on July 24, 2012 — Matt's birthday and the eighth anniversary of Maurice Carter's release from prison

It was three short months Maurice had been out of prison before his body succumbed to liver disease. But he savored every waking moment. Every bite of food, every beautiful view of nature, everything we take for granted on a daily basis was a true treat to Maurice.

Eight years later, take a brief moment to think of Maurice and remember two things. First, there are others still in prison. They're all God's children. Pray for them. Second, take a brief step back from your busy life and try to enjoy a day like Maurice did. We're all blessed. Life is good today.

Two souls meet for doughnuts, prayers

Each new customer who walks into Marge's Donut Den hears it from Marge herself in no uncertain terms: "Hey Al! You need this book!" "Hey young man, look what I have for you!"

Marge Wilson, longtime owner of Marge's Donut Den in Wyoming, has 100 copies of "Anthony's Prayers" stacked on a table. She is giving them away to her devoted customers this Friday morning with the zeal of a cheerful but determined evangelist.

Meanwhile, Anthony Torrone, the book's author, diligently signs each copy. Sometimes he adds a cartoon face for good measure. He signs one for 4-year-old Carson Hall, a cute little guy in Spider-Man boots.

"An author right here under our roof," marvels Carson's dad, Christopher Hall, the pastor of nearby Elevation Church. Carson puts $1 into a donation box Marge has set up for Anthony, who thanks the boy. "That will help me buy Lego sets at a special time," he says.

As anyone who has heard of Anthony knows, he is a prodigious builder of Lego creations – store signs, the Statue of Liberty, a giant paddle-wheeler, his late mother's headstone.

Marge wants to help Anthony build more. She also wants her customers to be inspired by the deep faith he expresses in "Anthony's Prayers." That's why she bought 500 copies to give away to anyone who walks through her door.

"He feels so blessed with what he has, and he shares so much with other people," Marge told me. "There's a lot of people like Anthony around. What if everybody just stretched out and helped their next-door neighbor?"

What if, indeed? And what if there were more people as generous of spirit as Marge and Anthony?

I've had the pleasure of writing about both of them before. In January 2013 I had the joy of seeing them meet due to a book I and others helped Anthony publish.

"Anthony's Prayers" is filled with his effusive thanks to God despite a life marked by hardship. He was abused at an institution for children with mental disabilities, teased for being different and lost his beloved mother in 1998. Yet his happy grin and mischievous quips are well-known in his West Side neighborhood.

Published in late 2011, the book features Anthony's writing, plus photos of him and his Legos. My former Press colleague Pat Shellenbarger and I edited the book while award-winning photographer Lance Wynn supplied most of the photos. This after Laura Hughes of Lowell, owner of Freeze Frame Publishing, offered to publish the volume at cost.

Anthony has that effect on people – just as he did on Marge Wilson, also a woman of strong faith.

"Be Kind, Be Good" reads a sign above the door at Marge's Donut Den, the bustling place at 1751 28th St. SW she opened in 1975. A big jar on the counter holds donations for the Samuel Omogo Foundation, a fund Marge set up to dig water wells in Nigeria.

Meanwhile, customers pile in, many walking out with big boxes full of glazed delight. Four women work the counter nonstop. It looks pretty much like it did about 25 years ago when I wrote about Marge for the old Wonderland magazine. Now as then, Marge lovingly presides over this community living room, where an engaged couple samples wedding cake and regulars chat over a tablecloth with their nicknames stitched on it.

This morning, the sign out front declares, "Meet a great man, Anthony, Friday 9 a.m." A little before 9 in walks Anthony with the Rev. Dick Ter Maat, his longtime friend and trustee of his trust fund. Marge hands Ter Maat a check for $4,000, and Anthony immediately signs a book for Marge.

"That's a very good picture of you, Anthony," she says, smiling. "Sure. That's right, Marge," he says, smiling back.

Marge loudly announces to the customers that Anthony's book is available for free, signed by him. "You will love it!" adds her sister, Marilyn Free, the general manager.

Anthony signs one for Gordie Amthor, a regular who opens Marge's mail each day.

"I thought this will make more people understand what a good father God is," Anthony says. Replies Marge, leaning close to him, "He intends for all of us to help each other."

He signs another for Tara Balzeski, one of the counter cashiers. "I'm a Lego builder," he tells her. "I am too!" she says. Later, she confesses she still has a case from childhood, adding, "When I get home, me and my son (Alex, 4) are going to look at this book."

Over at the regulars table with Bill the Golfer, Bob the Builder and Windmill Joe, Verna Magnuson leafs through the book. Her nickname on the tablecloth is "Trouble."

"I think it's wonderful," says Verna, 87, widow of former Wyoming Mayor Jack Magnuson. "He tells everything he's thankful for. In everyday life, we thank God for every little thing he does."

Joel Canales, an artist whose work hangs on Marge's wall, confides he's thankful for her. "If you were to line up the people she's helped here, it would go from here to Detroit," he tells me.

Meanwhile, Anthony's still signing books, Marge at his elbow. "Marge," he says to her, "do you think I could open up a bookstore in your room, called Marge's Bookstore?"

"No, because it should be all you," she chides him gently. "It's your talent."

Later, Anthony cracks to Verna Magnuson, "Doesn't Marge only look like she's 15?"

"He wanted to get his bases covered so he could get another doughnut," says Marge, 73.

Then, to Anthony: "Your message is so wonderful, that I thought everybody else should have it."

Jan. 16, 2013

An American Muslim serves his country

On Sept. 11, 2001, Jay Munir and I saw different skies, but we felt the same anger.

His sky was filled with black smoke billowing from the Pentagon, as he walked home after being evacuated from his Washington, D.C. law office.

Mine was spotless blue, a beautiful Grand Rapids day in all respects save one — the world had changed in a horrible way.

A decade later, I vividly remember my numb shock, racing fear and growing rage — how dare they do this to us? — as I ran about trying to register other people's feelings for The Grand Rapids Press. I didn't know what to do other than work my tail off and call my daughter at college to tell her I loved her.

As an American-born Muslim, Munir's emotions were both more complex and focused.

Walking home from his office near the White House, Munir saw the hellish evidence of American Airlines Flight 77's crash into the Pentagon. As his steps quickened, so did his anger at those responsible.

"We could see black smoke rising over the city," Munir told me from his office in Karachi, Pakistan. "That was the moment I knew I wanted to do something to serve."

Beyond the instinctive desire many Americans felt to do something, anything, Munir felt a special responsibility. Raised in Cascade Township, educated at Forest Hills, Yale and Harvard, fluent in French, Arabic and Urdu, Munir had both the skills and desire to help improve U.S. relations with the Muslim world.

Three years later, he joined the U.S. State Department. He has worked in Saudi Arabia, Paris, Iraq, Jordan, Tunisia, Syria and recently arrived in Pakistan, his parents' native land. He's chief of the political and economic section at the U.S. Consulate in Karachi, keeping in touch with key constituencies and explaining U.S. policy.

"Being an American has always been the most important thing to me," said Munir, 35. "I always felt a desire to give back for the opportunities America has given me."

In that, again, Jay and I are much the same.

In fact, we have found much in common over the years, chatting over coffee on his breaks from abroad. In our concern for promoting peace, tolerance and understanding, we share values that cut across our different faiths. We are Americans first and foremost.

I've been grateful to get to know Jay, as I have been to know his mother, Ghazala, for many years. His father, Mazhar, is a psychiatrist, and sister Reema a radiologist. Theirs is a kind, loving family much like my own. We share aspirations for a good life and a peaceful world. Their Islamic faith and our Christian tradition pose no obstacles to these shared values; in fact, it enhances them.

"We gather here as one American family," Ghazala said at an interfaith prayer service at St. Andrew's Cathedral on the night of the 9/11 attacks, summing up a grief that knew no creed.

Knowing Jay, Ghazala and other area Muslims has helped keep me grounded over the past 10 years. While a substantial minority of Americans worry about Muslims' loyalties and intentions, I have had the privilege of knowing people just as concerned about the safety and welfare of their country and families as I am.

Just knowing people personally, it seems, does a lot to counter the fear and insecurity that have pushed people apart post-9/11. In our age of airport pat-downs, political polarization and mosque protests, we need to know our neighbors before we can love them.

Researchers say knowing just one person of a different faith changes people's attitudes towards the whole religion. In a recent Wall Street Journal op-ed piece, scholars David Campbell and Robert Putnam argue friendship and marriage allayed historical suspicions by Protestants against Catholics and Jews.

The same may happen with Islam, they suggested; however, they reported only 7 percent of Americans are friends with a Muslim.

"Feeling warmly toward a given religion follows from having a close relationship with someone of that religion," the authors wrote.

Happily, West Michigan has an opportunity to get to know its neighbors of other faiths through the Year of Interfaith Understanding 2012. Key leaders launched the effort as a positive community response to the 10th anniversary of 9/11.

Meanwhile, Jay Munir is working hard to improve relations with Pakistan and promote America's image worldwide.

He emphasizes the opportunities America has provided Muslims, the help it has provided to Muslim-majority countries and the lives Americans have sacrificed fighting terrorism.

"We have a lot to be proud of. Our challenge is to be able to communicate that to people in this part of the world."

He also wants to communicate to Americans that terrorism threatens us all, including Muslims, and that American Muslims should "speak up loudly and often against terrorism and extremism." Al-Qaida gunmen killed five of his consulate colleagues in Saudi Arabia, and a Syrian friend of his was killed in pro-democracy protests.

His parents are proud of his work despite the risks. His patriotism has been evident since he eagerly studied U.S. history as a boy, Ghazala says: "We obviously worry, but then we know that he was destined for this important work."

When he left his post in Syria, a friend's mother told Jay, "I've always loved America, but after meeting you, I love it more."

The world seems darker and more dangerous since 9/11. It's hard to know what to do with our fears and anxieties. Perhaps just getting to know someone can help ease them — and show our love for America.

Sept. 10, 2011

Learning lessons from Tom

Driving westbound on Int. 196 I thought, I totally can't handle this day. It was midway through one of those all-stress all-the-time days. Tasks hurtled toward me as fast as the eastbound freeway cars, and deadlines closed in like that jerk in the mini-tank climbing up my bumper.

Then I thought of the wise advice of my friend, Tom Puksta. "Let the Lord have it," Tom would say. "Just say, 'I can't handle it, God. It's all yours.'"

I did that. In short order, my day improved immensely — a small miracle courtesy of a good man.

Tom used to invoke this miracle when he worked at American Seating, scheduling the production of school chairs and stadium seats. He often told me about his working days in long talks at his West Side home.

My family lived across the street from Tom during our first year in Grand Rapids. We were a long baseball toss away from John Ball Park and a short walk to Sacred Heart of Jesus Catholic Church, where my daughter went to kindergarten.

Tom and his late wife, Dorothy, were guardian angels as we got to know a new city. Their friendly hospitality helped assure us we had come to a good place where neighbors cared for each other.

When we moved a mile away, I stayed in touch with Tom. I dropped by from time to time to shoot the breeze. Tom always welcomed me with a cold can of Coke and bade me goodbye with a big hug.

It was a comforting place to go, one of those working-class West Side homes with a wide front porch and lace curtains. Pictures of Tom's kids and grandkids dominated the decor. Sometimes the Tigers were on TV.

In his dining room hung a comforting sign. It read something like, "Good morning. This is God. I will be handling all of your problems today. Have a good day."

Tom wears his faith like a comfortable cardigan. He would never push it on you. He would see that as un-Christian. He just offers it to you, like a can of Coke.

We would talk about faith sometimes, about the weird ways God has of making things come out right. But mostly we would just talk about our families, Grand Rapids and the wonderful life he has lived.

He enriched me with stories of falling in love with Dorothy when she was a schoolgirl, working in the old downtown movie theaters and raising his four children.

I write about Tom now because earlier this fall he had to leave his home. He took up brief residence at Saint Mary's Health Care, where he was diagnosed with pancreatic cancer.

At age 90, that translated into months, weeks, perhaps days to live.

Tom is now at a retirement residence. He lives out his days attended by Hospice nurses and visited by loved ones — of whom there are many.

Some are former neighbors like me. Tom's neighbors have cut his grass and shoveled his drive for years. Those who move out make sure the new ones agree to do that. He has that effect on people.

These days when I visit, Tom and I talk a little more about faith. His seems to grow stronger as his days grow shorter.

I listen with quiet amazement as Tom talks of reaching the end of his life.

He wonders when God will choose to take him, and why he's still here in a weakening body.

"There must be a reason," he says with full confidence.

I'm sure he has his dark nights, but I don't detect much fear in Tom. He seems ready at any time to join Dorothy, say good-bye to his wonderful family and hello to God.

"I've turned it all over to him," Tom tells me. "I'm at peace with the world. I know he's with me, so there's no problem."

I think that's the reason you're still here, Tom — to teach the rest of us faith.

Dec. 11, 2004

From the father to the son

Jeff Thomas is telling me about a nonprofit he heads that aims to help other nonprofits find new ways to meet human need, especially hunger. Ending the latter was a passion for his father, John Arnold, a national food banking pioneer who died March 25 at age 61.

Suddenly, Jeff leans forward over the dining room table, raises his voice a bit and for a moment seems to become his father.

"We know for a FACT that there is so much low-hanging fruit there," declares Jeff, 25, with the same articulate intensity I'd heard from John many times. "Your typical community in America is already spending enough money on hunger to solve the problem of hunger if they were doing it with optimum efficiency."

"Like father, like son" doesn't begin to capture the seamless integrity with which Jeff has carried on the work and ideas of his dad. For one thing, his voice sounds so much like John's that phone callers used to mix them up when Jeff was an intern at Feeding America West Michigan, the Comstock Park food bank Arnold headed for 21 years.

More importantly, Jeff not only took the baton when John had finished his leg of the race, he works to find new approaches to hunger and other social ills. He does this along with his wife, Elianna Bootzin, executive administrative assistant at Feeding America West Michigan.

The beauty of a person like John Arnold is how his example continues to inspire others long after his work has ended – including his son, who takes up the cause with renewed energy.

John helped create one of the country's most productive food banks, serving more than 100,000 households in 40 counties, while leading the way nationally in practices such as mobile food pantries and letting clients choose their own food.

Instead of holding a memorial service for him, Arnold invited people to perform activities such as donating to the food bank's endowment fund, picking up trash or giving blood. He was one of the more dedicated public servants I have known, bringing to his work a combination of Quaker and Buddhist philosophy and good old '60s Sixties radical idealism.

A revealing glimpse into his thinking can be found in "Peacemaking Under Fire," a book he wrote last year while battling prostate cancer. In it he tells of his decision to enroll in the Marines in order to help end to the Vietnam War. His antiwar friends thought he was nuts, but Arnold believed it was the only way to tell the truth regardless of the obvious risk to himself.

"(I)t is far better to live for something, to have one's life have meaning, than to slink away and hide from what needs to be done," Arnold wrote.

He seems to have successfully passed that conviction onto Jeff, along with Jeff's mother, Jeanne Thomas, who was married to John for 37 years.

While at City Middle School, Jeff drew up a national map and directory of U.S. food banks that was widely used. In high school, he made a video of his father promoting mobile food pantries on beverage trucks, now a widespread method nationally.

As a college intern, Jeff also improved the food bank website and wrote a condensed version of John's manifesto, "Charity Food Programs That Can End Hunger in America."

Arnold really believed hunger can be ended, and Jeff does, too. They talked about that and other things on yearly trips around the country, visiting food banks and historic Civil War sites.

A few years ago, they talked about forming a nonprofit that could explore new ideas for better human service without spending more money. The result was Nonprofit Innovations, a 501 (c) (3) of which Jeff is executive director. Among its projects: findafoodpantry.org, a directory of more than 10,000 pantries across the U.S.

Jeff also re-tells the stories, with relish and sometimes with tears, that John told to illustrate how one person, donation or instance of serendipity could make a big difference. One such: John convinced a reluctant food pantry director to take a load of newly donated fresh cranberries. Soon after, a client came to that pantry needing boiled cranberries to help treat her daughter's illness.

Jeff and Elianna are creating an online archive of these teaching stories, so that Arnold's ideas can reach more people.

Arnold kept reaching people up to the end. Even as he was in hospice care at home, he published an essay in The Press emphasizing the importance of nutrition to children's well-being, and how we already have the resources we need if we just used them more efficiently.

Jeff learned those lessons as a child, helping his dad clean up trash off the Lake Michigan beach, then watching others start picking it up, too. That was typically how Arnold got things done, Jeff says: By seeing a need, then acting on it.

"'They need to' would invariably turn into 'I need to,'" Jeff says, wiping away tears.

How wonderful if "I need to" turned into "we all need to."

May 14, 2012

Gene made this a better place

When it came time to pay final respects to Gene Proctor, Grand Rapids just kept walking in the door

There was Sister Mary Aquinas Weber, the Dominican nun and former Aquinas College administrator. And there were the Revs. Reggie Smith, Nathaniel Moody and Arthur Bailey.

Also coming into the Gillespie Memorial Chapel this day were Peter Cook, businessman and philanthropist; former City Commissioner Bill Blickley; and, holding court in the front foyer, Proctor's close friend Reuben Smartt, who welcomed most everyone with a ready laugh and a good story.

This is community, our community. Gene Proctor would have loved every minute, because Gene dedicated most of his 74 years to building community.

"His passion was with the community, building bridges," said Tim Proctor, one of Gene and Virginia Proctor's seven children. "That's where his heart was."

Oh, yes. Gene's heart was with Grand Rapids. Thanks to Gene, we are a little closer than we would have been without him. Blacks and whites know each other a little better. And all of us pay a little more attention to children.

His recent passing seemed so sudden. His friends and loved ones knew he had been in poor health for some time. For the rest of us, it was a sudden intake of breath: Oh no, not Gene!

It was like waking up to find the corner church was torn down overnight.

Gene Proctor was a walking institution, a grace-filled embodiment of Grand Rapids' best qualities. It is hard to imagine this city without him.

But that is what we have today. So now we must turn our imaginations to how we can build community as Gene did: breaking down barriers, building bridges, teaching children.

Gene did all that with a matchless smile and a nagging limp, the result of a car accident about 50 years ago. The doctors thought he had died. But Gene still had way too much to give.

He had yet to help start Camp Tall Turf, a Christian retreat near Hesperia where the Proctor Youth and Family Center sits among towering pines.

He had yet to run the Baxter Community Center, a haven of health and recreation for thousands of inner-city kids. He had yet to become executive director of the D&W Foundation.

And if you needed someone to raise money, Gene was your man. He once got Cook and Rich DeVos to contribute $100,000 on the same night. The Grand Rapids Community Foundation last year named him an outstanding African American philanthropist.

"He liked everybody, and everybody liked him," Cook said outside the funeral home. "He was just a good citizen."

Gene's unfailing cheerfulness was no act, his daughter Elizabeth said: "That's just the way he was. He was our hero."

Sister Aquinas called him "one of those stalwart people."

"There was a gentleness about him, and a real caring for Grand Rapids."

Smartt joked he was the liberal Democrat to Gene's conservative Republican. They were founding Tall Turf board members and longtime friends.

"I never saw him cross," Smartt said. "If something bothered him, he came out with something positive."

It was always a pleasure to run into Gene, whether in a boardroom or a bathroom. He was one of Grand Rapids' good guys, grace with a limp.

He and his wife bought a home last year in Woodland Park, where they grew up and met.

Gene got to spend one last summer near his boyhood home before God took him to his eternal one.

Gene died peacefully in his sleep. He looked that way at the funeral home, asleep in peace, dressed in a sharp tie.

I will miss you, Gene. We all will. Grand Rapids won't be the same without you, but it is better because of you.

March 31, 2007

Sister nears the end in peace

It's a fair day on the green grounds of Marywood, home to about 125 Dominican sisters. A slight breeze cools the midday summer air. In the shade of the courtyard, a nun walks up to Sister Rose Miriam Visner and hugs her.

Sister Marie Rosaire Longtin, 86, congratulates Sister Rose Miriam on her 100th birthday, which she celebrates this day.

"Each day, you're glad you're living," Sister Rose Miriam answers in a soft, soft voice. "Sure. That's the way it goes." She laughs.

So it goes for Sister Rose Miriam, living out her days among her beloved sisters in faith, completing a life she chose in 1924 instead of becoming a Broadway dancer.

I can't picture her then, a young girl working in Chicago, forsaking the stage for a life of devotion. But I see her almost magically clear now, a tiny woman in a wheelchair, making me notice the beauty all around us.

Her hair is fine and white. She wears a green-and-white dress and a turquoise scarf. A purple-beaded rosary hangs around her neck.

"It's a nice place to end my days," she says, thinking of her daily prayers, and the friends who read to her at night, and the women who take her outside to drink in God's nature.

"It's really a wonderful way to end life. I'm very calm. I enjoy very much what God has given me."

Then she talks of seeing hungry, poor women, trudging through downtown streets on their way to scrubbing offices.

"None of us should have that," she says sadly. "We should have an ending of life that is pleasant, and that's what I have."

As she talks, a quiet amazement overcomes me. It's the same feeling I received when I first met Sister Rose Miriam four years ago. It comes from witnessing someone so utterly at peace with herself. She looks back at her long life with a smile and no hint of regret.

There is joy, too, in seeing a long life well lived, coming to its contented conclusion.

Surely that's the way it's meant to be, despite countless cruel examples to the contrary.

A few days earlier, I had spoken with a friend on his way to a funeral. The deceased was a loving father of two, creator of a hospital charity, fully in the midst of a good life. On a boat with his family, he fell dead of a heart attack at age 47. Bam.

Where's the fairness in that? You can drive yourself crazy with the question. Or you can take it as given that life is unfair. The best you can do is live it lovingly.

Sister Rose Miriam enjoys simple things, like having someone read to her about Joan of Arc or Catherine of Siena.

When she was a child on Spencer Street NE in Grand Rapids, she enjoyed playing croquet and taking walks on Saturdays past the millionaires' homes.

"We thought it was wonderful to see those great, rich houses."

Since then, she has seen the sinking of the Titanic, two world wars, the Depression and the deaths of five sisters, three of whom were nuns, too. Three brothers also died, at birth or soon after.

She filled her life with the joys of teaching, sisterhood and prayer. What has she learned about God? I ask.

"We don't have to learn, really," she answers. "It just grows in you. You understand that, don't you? You become what you might call godly."

Are you ready to meet God? I ask.

"You never wish to die, but when I die, I'd call it a pleasure," she says, with that same disarming calm. "It may be there will be a little suffering to walk all the way at the end. But when we die, it's going to be God."

And life? With all its suffering and strife, what about life?

"It's been beautiful," she says. "Not only beautiful here, but all my life."

Her soft words graced the warm air, and hung there like a prayer.

Aug. 16, 2003

Second Inning

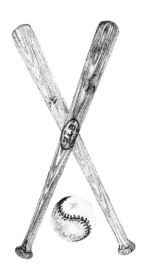

Play Ball!

The perfect imperfect game

In the beginning was the ball, and the ball was with a boy, and the boy threw it to his father. And the father said, "Nice toss." And he threw it back to his son.

Then he said, "Now, try holding it with your first two fingers along that seam. Yeah, just like that. Now when you throw it, try snapping your wrist a little, like so. To make it spin and curve."

The son tried throwing it like that, but the ball did not curve. It hit the dirt and went bouncing past his father.

"That's OK," his dad said. "Try it again."

So the boy tried it again and again, over many days. Until one day, the ball curved.

And the dad said, "Atta boy!" And the son felt perfectly proud.

That's how my dad taught me the curve ball, more or less, in the yard. Over long summer afternoons, Dad also taught me the fastball and the changeup, passing along pitching mysteries he had learned as a child.

The curve was my favorite. I tried to perfect the pitch, a round arc that started toward the batter's head and ended at the far lower reach of his bat. One dusty afternoon, I struck out many Little League batters with that curve.

But other afternoons I couldn't get the ball over the plate. When I did, the batters hammered it beyond left field. Such is the mystery of baseball — which is to say the puzzle of life.

One day everything goes well, and you look up at a perfect blue sky and say, "Thank you, God." The next, everything you touch breaks, it's unbearably muggy and you wonder just how it is you ticked off God.

This is one of the many things my dad taught me through baseball. You'll have your good days and bad. You'll win some and lose a lot. And no matter how good you are, someone will always be better.

This helps explain the extraordinary drama surrounding the recent perfect-yet-not game pitched by Armando Galarraga of the Detroit Tigers. Mysteriously, this sometimes good but never great pitcher couldn't miss the strike zone that day. He was just one out away from doing something done only 20 times in baseball history: retire all 27 batters.

Then, umpire Jim Joyce called the very last batter safe at first, and the crowd gasped. A veteran ump who had made the right calls for years made Galarraga's perfect game a mere one-hitter with one wrong call. The imperfection lay not with Galarraga, but with Joyce.

But it the end, the whole thing turned out to be perfect, after all.

In his tearful apologies for getting it wrong, Joyce was a heartbreaking figure of repentance. In Galarraga's gracious handshake with Joyce the next day, and his teammates' gentle pats on his shoulder, we saw forgiveness at its best.

"Hey, we all make mistakes," they were saying. "We're all human. Don't beat yourself up over it." It was a perfect picture of grace.

"There's no crying in baseball!" Tom Hanks declared in "A League of Their Own." He was wrong. Jim Joyce's tears quieted the angry shouts of outraged fans and fuming pundits.

My father is not perfect, nor are all the other fathers who will get their due recognition tomorrow on Father's Day. But they pass along precious mysteries to their sons and daughters, be it a curve ball, how to bait a hook or cook a delicious breakfast.

And though I will always admire my father as the man I would like to be, he will never let me beat myself up for my imperfections. He will put his hand on my shoulder and say, "Hey, we all make mistakes. We're all human."

And even though neither one of us can throw it any longer, the curve ball flies between us, hitting the mitt with a pop as sweet as love.

June 19, 2010

Finding the divine in the ordinary

A s I glide down Mount Mercy Drive on my bicycle, there's always that moment of anticipation: Have the ghosts come out of the cornfield tonight?

Then, turning the curve, he comes into view behind the trees: the rightfielder, poised to go after a fly ball in the wide, green expanse of Sullivan Field.

Ah, my heart says, there's a game.

So I sweep down onto Valley Avenue NW, past the green grandstand and into the gravel surrounding the diamond. Pick up a lemonade at the concession stand. Sit in the wooden bleachers, in the cool of the overhang, and watch the young men play ball. With probably the same silly smile plastered on my face as Kevin Costner wore in "Field of Dreams," when the spirits of dead guys came out of an Iowa cornfield for the sheer joy of playing baseball.

This is high summer: fastball smacking the catcher's mitt, shortstop kicking up dust, rightfielder running across the green field, playing an always green game.

Green, the color of ordinary time.

We are in ordinary time, that blissfully noneventful period of the Christian calendar between Pentecost and Advent. The longest season of the year. No big festivals coming up. Just a wide expanse of plain old time, days upon days of living regular life.

Give me the joy of the ordinary.

The HarperCollins Encyclopedia of Catholicism calls it "time ordered for, or ordained to, the everyday living of a Christian life." In Latin, it is referred to as tempus ordinarium, meaning "measured time."

That says it nicely: a time for measured life, purposeful activities wisely mingled with utter laziness. Not the time when each day is 24 hours less to get ready for Christmas. In ordinary time, days breathe and weeks last a little longer.

These days Christians pay more attention to ordinary time, as they do to the whole liturgical calendar. But some may not be all that sure about what "ordinary" means, except a time when church committees let up for awhile.

What used to be, for Protestants, considered part of Pentecost is still a significant time of growth, if you ask the Rev. Tom Schwanda, a Reformed Church teacher and spiritual retreat leader. Schwanda calls it a time when "God meets you in the ordinary details and routines of life."

"It's in the ruts, the highs and lows," Schwanda says. "Not always the spectacular ah-ha's. It's just being faithful in whatever we do."

That sounds easier than it is. Americans like the spectacular stuff: spiritual revelations, mountaintop experiences, movies that make you cry, Cedar Point. But if that's all there is, things can get pretty dry in between.

What about puttering around the yard? That's where Schwanda likes to meet God, landscaping his lawn.

There also may be some ordered purpose in painting a porch railing. You have no choice but to paint slowly and patiently, leaving large unoccupied spaces of your mind open to possibly useful thoughts. Or watching the sky turn twilight, or feeling the wind off Lake Michigan.

Can one downshift enough to think, see, feel these ordinary marvels?

On certain golden evenings, I like to meet up with the divine down at Sullivan Field.

It's difficult to find a more measured game than baseball. There's purity and grace in the pitcher's motion, the hook of a curve ball and the astounding arc of a line drive. The kind of thing only people could think up, and play as if it had meaning.

What we used to call Valley Field is somehow not time-bound. Shrouded by trees, enclosed by fence, it's a place where kids can chase foul balls without fear, and fans can chat in the shade while the game flows smoothly. Before them spreads a green diamond, refracting something good and true about the plain pleasure of being alive.

It brings back something of the times I remember as a child, going to fast-pitch softball games in Detroit with my grandparents. Magic was there, too, in the intense skill yet utter nonchalance of the players, ordinary men with extraordinary talents.

True, baseball is not life. But like the well-tended garden, it is wonderfully ordinary, and for fans, divinely ordained.

I have to wonder: Can you find God in a perfectly executed bunt?

July 18, 1998

Cubs heap their sins on scapegoat

I thought I was just watching a baseball game. But lo and behold, I saw someone tear the very fabric of the universe. And what a sickening sight it was.

It was seemingly torn by Steve Bartman, that poor, sorry sucker who reached up for a foul fly ball in game 6 of the Cubs-Marlins playoff series. He was the bespectacled guy in the Cubs cap who could only see that ball coming down — to him, at such a historic moment, with his beloved Cubbies just five outs away from the World Series!

Apparently, neither this front-row fan, nor the several spectators stretching out their arms around him, could see leftfielder Moises Alou, whose outstretched glove was just inches from the ball when this unluckiest of fans deflected the ball with his outstretched hand.

Then it all came apart — the Cubs' seemingly sure victory, their entry into their first World Series in 58 years, the chance to win their first championship in nearly a century.

Back came the Cubs Curse, settling over the stunned crowd like the flashback of a 3 a.m. nightmare. Some trace that curse back to 1945, when a tavern owner reportedly hexed the ballpark after being denied entry to a World Series game with his goat.

But wait — did Steve Bartman start the cosmic tear that unraveled the Cubs? Or has he been heaped with scorn and driven into hiding by another kind of curse — the curse of being the scapegoat?

Yes, I was furious at the guy, and all the other fans who interfered with Alou's almost-sure catch. But you know what? I might have done the very same thing, had that ball been coming down to me.

I shouldn't have, nor any fan fully paying attention to the game. But the moment is huge, the adrenaline pumping, and all you see is that ball coming to YOU! Bartman said as much in a moving apology issued from the shadows:

"I am so truly sorry from the bottom of this Cub fan's broken heart."

Spoken like a guy who grew up fielding flies hit by his father and who now coaches a youth baseball team.

The Rev. Paul Krupinski feels for him.

"As a kid growing up, when I went to the ballpark, aside from the victory, that was the one thing I hoped happened: Hit one near me. He just did the normal, natural, human thing," says Krupinski, pastor of Trinity Lutheran Church.

Krupinski has standing to speak. He grew up on Chicago's Northwest Side and is a lifelong Cubs fan. Krupinski is plenty broken up about the Cubs' collapse. But he doesn't blame Bartman.

"I felt for him, the way he was treated. It's not what we would call in the church 'Christian.' The poor kid ... he probably has to move to Albuquerque just to begin a new life."

Bartman and his unlucky moment, replayed ad nauseum on video and photo, has become the scapegoat for the frustration and anger seething through Cub Nation, Krupinski says.

It's a common human tendency all the way back to the Bible. God commanded Aaron to sacrifice one goat to him and send a scapegoat into the desert to symbolically carry away humanity's sins.

Are we going to exile Steve Bartman to the desert because he did the same thing many of us easily could have done? Plaster his name, address and phone number all over the Internet because he did something so maddeningly and typically human?

Speaking of maddeningly and typically human, it's really the Cubs who messed up here, under enormous psychological pressure.

It is they who, after a couple terrible breaks, collapsed before the horrified eyes of millions who regard them as a national treasure — a cursed national treasure. We need to cut these guys a break.

Yes, it's heartbreaking. But for crying out loud, this is baseball, not a plague of locusts.

I'm as guilty as the next fanatic of investing too many hopes and dreams in this great game. At times like these, I remind myself it's still a bunch of millionaires throwing a ball around. And forget blaming Steve Bartman. The guy already feels miserable.

If you get his address via email, send him a get-well card. Say something to him that you would want someone to say to you.

Then trying walking 90 feet in his baseball cleats, all alone, and see how that feels.

Oct. 18, 2003

Taste of victory, grace of defeat

The high morning sun beat down as the Cheetahs took the field. It was the last inning of the last game of my last season as coach of this scrappy city league team, and we were winning.

This was something new. We had not won a game all season. We had almost won a few times, but invariably found a way to lose.

Through missed chances, bad luck or worse coaching, we had booted away opportunities to celebrate with an extra-big Dairy Queen sundae.

Through it all I kept thinking, we can't lose every game. Even the 1962 Mets didn't lose every game.

I racked my brain, fiddled with the lineup and pretended it wasn't that big a deal.

As the Cheetahs took the field, our chances seemed auspicious. We were playing well. We were two runs up.

"Go get 'em, buddy," I told my son, Max, as he walked to the pitcher's mound.

There is simply no doubt baseball is the cruelest sport of all.

Other games -— basketball, football, soccer — you're just part of the arms and legs.

You make a mistake, then seconds later you become part of the blur and the fans are diverted by new action.

In baseball, a mistake lasts forever. You drop a fly ball with the bases loaded, then stand there naked in front of God and everybody.

It's like Pavarotti's voice has cracked in the middle of an aria. There is nowhere to hide.

Plus, it is so blamed difficult. Ever try to hit an 80-mph fastball? Ridiculous. It's almost as hard as getting the ball over the plate from 60 feet, 6 inches away. Fielders must constantly be thinking, yet long spells of inaction lull them to sleep.

So if baseball is so ruthless, why is it so romanticized? Egg-headed writers rhapsodize about its elegance. Criminy, you'd think it was ballet or something.

I don't know the answer. But there is something about base-ball that goes beyond the physical beauty of the game. It plays out in long, slow dramas where weaknesses show and skills shine. Its players toil through long, hot seasons, and in the end, almost all of them lose.

Out of more than 700 big-league players, only two dozen of them get what all of them want: a World Series ring.

There is something especially heartbreaking about baseball, which is perhaps why it is so easy to relate to. I remember lis-tening to a Detroit Tigers game back in 1961, when they were battling the Yankees for the pennant. Don Mossi gave up only one run, and lost. "A heartbreaker," my dad called it, and I felt it.

Heck, Harvey Haddix once pitched 12 perfect innings — not one man reached first base — then lost in the 13th. *Perfect*, and it wasn't good enough.

As any Cubs fan can tell you — and these days, any Tigers fan — there is a sad sweetness to losing in baseball. Roger Kahn put it this way, in writing about his beloved Brooklyn Dodgers in "The Boys of Summer":

"You may glory in a team triumphant, but you fall in love with a team in defeat."

We all know the pain of defeat on a regular basis. We feel its sting in snubs, lost opportunities, layoffs and divorces. The pain lingers. Mistakes seem to last forever.

With baseball, you absorb the pain of losing through a lovely game, where even in defeat the players exhibit extraordinary skills of hand and eye.

For the player, the pain of a botched fly ball suddenly is obliterated when you fire a perfect throw to third to cut down the baserunner — an amazing feat, unthinkingly executed.

For the fan, defeats don't dim the glory of the game, or the long, slow pleasure of watching players perform marvels born of tireless practice and their God-given abilities. To lose is no true loss, for the boys have played a great game.

The Cheetahs lost. Max did not pitch poorly, nor did any other Cheetah play badly. A hit, a walk, an off-line throw was all it took for things to unravel. Due to league rules, they had to play out the inning even after they had lost. They stood in the hot sun, totally dispirited.

Then, the miracle. One by one, their parents stood up and cheered. Well done, boys, they cheered. It felt like a spray of cool water on their sweat-soaked faces. It was the sound of grace.

The boys came off the field, winners every one.

June 22, 2002

Now batting, Father Steve 'Crash' Cron

Many have known the Rev. Steve Cron as an excellent priest down through the years. But did you know he's also a primo ballplayer?

Hey, it says so right on his baseball card. In his 2004 and 2009 trips to the Detroit Tigers Fantasy Camp, Father Cron has batted a cool .400, including a triple and four RBIs. The southpaw has even made a few trips to the pitcher's mound, although his 5.58 ERA is not quite so distinguished.

I hereby christen him "Crash" Cron. That's a nod not just to his hitting prowess but to his boyhood Tigers hero, "Stormin' Norman" Cash, whose No. 25 Cron wears on his two Tigers jerseys.

Crash Cron wears the jersey smartly on his fantasy camp baseball card, which he's distributed to eager kids during his six trips to Havana. In Cuba, as in other parts of Latin America, the youth are even more avid about baseball than here, where football, basketball and hockey vie for their attention.

Cron, you see, is not only devoted to the Lord but to the great game of baseball. He is particularly fascinated by Latin American ballplayers, who are favorites of many of his Latino parishioners at St. Joseph the Worker Catholic Church in Wyoming. He has taught two courses on Latinos in baseball for Grand Valley State University.

Latino ballplayers have rejuvenated our great game, in this fan's humble opinion. Just look at our beloved Tigers: Martinez, Avila, Infante, Iglesias, and, of course, the mighty Miguel Cabrera. I've rooted them on in packed games at Comerica Park, where I once ran into Father Cron, scorecard in hand, just a few seats away.

As the Tigers close in (we hope) on another division title on their way to (we pray) another World Series, it is mighty Miguel and the other Latino stars leading the way. As of Monday, Cabrera not only led the major leagues in batting average, slugging percentage and RBIs, but was still playing with boyish joy despite chronic injuries in a grueling pennant drive.

"Look at how much fun he's having," Cron marvels. "He's hurting, makes millions and has nothing left to prove, and is just plain having a ball. Just grateful to be here – this is fun!"

That passion for the game, flair for flash and sheer excellence are some of what Latino players have brought to our national pastime. As of Opening Day, about 24 percent of Major League ballplayers were born in Latin America, according to Fox News Latino.

For Cron, his love of baseball, the church and Latin Americans are natural outgrowths of his childhood in Carson City. He grew up in that small Montcalm County town worshipping at St. Mary Parish. He so wanted to be a priest that his grandmother made him an altar one Christmas.

Young Steve also worshipped the Tigers, following the feats of Cash, Rocky Colavito and Al Kaline via the broadcasts of the legendary Ernie Harwell. When he wasn't tuned in to Harwell's comforting play-by-play he was either playing sandlot baseball or pretend priest.

On June 17, 1962, he went to his first game at the cathedral of Tiger Stadium. His pastor, the Rev. Ralph Kelly, sent him and other altar boys to see a doubleheader with the Boston Red Sox, a ritual repeated each summer. (Last year on Father's Day, he marked that game's 50th anniversary with a game at Comerica Park, where he caught his first-ever foul ball.)

Meanwhile, the young fan had begun taking Spanish classes in seventh grade, prompting Father Kelly to enlist him to help with Masses for migrant workers. A seminarian, Larry Hartwig, took him to assist at migrant camps, and later encouraged him to live and work among migrants while Cron was in seminary.

Thus was born Cron's lifelong ministry, which has included two tenures at St. Joseph the Worker, and which in no way has diminished his devotion to baseball. He has attended 35 Opening Days, all home games of the 1984 and 2006 World Series, and has kept a written record of every Tigers game since 1969: 7,145 of them as of Sunday. Now that's religious devotion.

What so powerfully draws a priest to baseball? Its timelessness — no clock ends the game — its rich history, its human imperfections and even its scriptural overtones: "In the big inning, God created the heavens and the earth," Cron quips. The very point of the game could be a sermon theme.

"You start at home," Cron says. "What's your goal? Get back home. The game of life is getting back where we started from."

He owns a set of rosary beads linked by baseballs. He's not above praying with them during times of Tigers duress.

"I got this the year the Tigers were losing 119 games," he says with a knowing smile. "I used it a lot."

His deep research on Latino ballplayers has unearthed fascinating facts. Long before Jackie Robinson broke the color barrier for African American players in 1947, two Cubans, Armando Marsans and Rafael Almeida, played for the 1911 Cincinnati Reds. Their light skin allowed them to be passed off by baseball bigwigs as white Spaniards "pure as Castilian soap."

The Washington Senators recruited many Latino players as cheap labor while the stars were off fighting in World War II. Soon, big-league rosters were populated by the likes of Luis Aparicio, Orlando Cepeda and the great Alou brothers, Felipe, Matty and Jesus.

But this is now, and Cron's Hispanic parishioners fervently root for the Tigers and their Latino stars, as does he. He plans to take his granddaughter Jasmine — daughter of his adopted son Armondo — to see the Tigers play Seattle for her 10th birthday – as he has done for three other granddaughters.

"It warms my heart," he says. "They know I love baseball and the Tigers, and they get to go with me to a game they don't understand."

Father Steve clearly understands baseball — which, as we fans know, goes a long way toward understanding life.

Sept. 16, 2013

These sisters are faithful Tigers fans

Among the legions cheering them on toward a pennant, the Detroit Tigers have three especially devout fans in their corner.

"Good, good, good!" exclaims Sister Vita, clapping her hands as Miguel Cabrera launches a mighty home run.

"He's got some power!" adds Sister Janet, beaming at the television with a Madonna and baby Jesus statue on top.

Dominican Sisters Janet Brown, Vita Licari and Phyllis Mrozinski faithfully root for their team to make the playoffs as the regular season enters its final week. They're not wishing for divine intervention so much as timely hitting.

"They've faced some excellent pitchers, so they're not getting that ball to that bat," laments Sister Vita, all too accurately.

"They're leaving all those men on base," adds Sister Janet, who clearly reads her box scores.

As for Sister Phyllis, she admits she's not above ducking out of the community TV room to pray for help.

"When there's a pitching change, I'll go to my room and say, 'Oh, let the Tigers win!'"

Keep those prayers coming, sister. Monday we play the Twins.

These three are by no means the only Dominican sisters pulling for the Tigers. Several faithfully tune in to follow the boys as they vie for the playoffs and a return to the World Series they so meekly lost in 2006.

Seven gathered this night to watch the Tigers rout the Cleveland Indians, 11-3, including Sister Mario Pavoni wearing a Brandon Inge jersey.

It is good to have Catholic nuns on your side when you're down to the wire. If a bad hop can change the course of a game, can a Hail Mary hurt?

Playoffs or no, how fortunate Michigan is to have our Tigers in the hunt. When you lead the nation in unemployment, it's a blessing to also hold first place in the AL Central.

It's a blessing as well to have Ernie Harwell along for the ride. The longtime Tigers announcer's courageous acceptance of his inoperable cancer lends a poignancy to this season for those who fell asleep with his soothing voice in their ears.

I was lucky enough to be at Comerica Park when Ernie bid us a sweet and brief farewell. A man of deep and quiet faith, he spoke warmly of Michiganders' grit and family values, and of how "the good Lord has blessed me with a great journey."

His grace and gratitude moved Sister Phyllis: "He made you feel that way — gratitude, for life itself."

She and her fellow sisters are grateful for the joy baseball has given them in life.

Sister Janet grew up in a family of Tigers fans. Her dad would stay glued to the game even if they were down 10-1 with dinner waiting, hoping "they might win with the last pitch."

Sister Vita played street ball on the Southwest Side while her sisters played on a team called the Sodality Girls. They were organized by a fervent fan who lives at Marywood, Sister Lourdes Palazzolo.

Dominican Sisters formed teams in the '50s and '60s, playing games behind the Marywood Motherhouse. "We'd play ball after supper until the bell rang for prayers at 7 o'clock," Sister Phyllis recalls with a laugh.

So what is it about baseball that draws women of prayer?

"It's a nonviolent game," muses Sister Phyllis. "It's a relaxing game, but there's a lot of anticipation at the same time."

For Sister Janet, baseball is just great fun — which she believes is part of God's design.

"I believe in work, prayer, having fun," she says, ticking them off on her fingers. "I believe part of wholeness is to have fun in life. That makes us holy, too."

The sisters have fun following their favorite Tigers. Sister Vita's is Brandon Inge, "a very good man and a wonderful third baseman."

And God, does he enjoy a good Tigers game? You betcha, says Sister Phyllis.

"That's God's stage, the baseball diamond," she says with a smile. "God's right there, with each one of those guys. They'd lose every game if God wasn't there."

In fact, one sister pointed out to me God was a fan from the very start: "In the big inning, God created the heavens and the earth."

Let's hope God stays awake for those Twins games.

Sept. 26, 2009

Play ball on Sunday? Say it ain't so!

He had a terrific fastball.

That's what former Calvin College President William Spoelhof remembers most clearly about Johnny Vander Meer. It's probably what most people who saw Vander Meer would recall of the only major-league pitcher to throw two consecutive no-hitters.

But unlike most fans, Spoelhof recalls Vander Meer as a teen on the diamonds of Paterson, N.J. That's where Spoelhof grew up, while Vander Meer lived in neighboring Midland Park and played for that town's semi-pro Rangers.

The elderly scholar and the late ballplayer share interesting roots. Both had fathers who worked in the silk mills. Both avidly played baseball in those tough factory towns and both grew up in the Christian Reformed Church.

What does his CRC upbringing have to do with Johnny Vander Meer's baseball glory? More than you might think. The faith of "the Dutch Master" was strong, but cost him something dear in the pursuit of his God-given talent.

Vander Meer's name came up following the June 12 no-hitter thrown by Detroit Tigers pitcher Justin Verlander. Before Verlander's next start, sportswriters asked: Can he duplicate Vander Meer's fabulous feat?

He did not. But the Tigers fireballer has achieved stardom at age 24, as Vander Meer did at 23. Verlander likely will pitch in Tuesday's All-Star Game, as Vander Meer did in 1938, the year he made baseball history.

The young phenom for the Cincinnati Reds, who struck out batters ruthlessly and walked almost as many, already had no-hit the Boston Bees on Saturday, June 11, when he went to the mound four days later against the Brooklyn Dodgers.

The air was electric in the first night game ever played at Ebbets Field. Almost 39,000 fans, including about 700 of Vander Meer's family and friends from Midland Park, saw a fireworks display, a sprinting exhibition by Jesse Owens and a pre-game presentation of a watch to the handsome hurler.

With his Dutch-born parents in the stands, Vander Meer responded by throwing yet another no-hitter — a record as likely to be surpassed as a second parting of the Red Sea.

"It was quite a night," recalls his sister, Garberdina Nywening, a high schooler at the time who watched the game with her folks and Vander Meer's future wife.

However, not everyone back in Midland Park was so thrilled — particularly not at Vander Meer's church, Midland Park CRC. Since turning pro, Vander Meer had played ball on Sundays, a practice frowned upon by CRC doctrine of his day.

Vander Meer was forced early in his career to choose between the calling of his gifted left arm and a church tradition that considered Sabbath sport sinful.

The prevailing CRC view was neatly summed up by a 1921 poem in the denominational magazine, The Banner:

"Is it wrong to see a ball game on a Sunday afternoon, just to see skilled, clean enjoyment while the band strikes up a tune?" The Banner's terse answer: "Such things our Lord would never do." It referenced God's warning in Isaiah 58:13 against "doing as you please on my holy day."

"Doing as you please" included golf, fishing and most jobs. As for baseball, "Even baseball fans who wished to listen to radio broadcasts or reports of the games were urged to abstain on Sunday," according to a 1990 article in Origins, a publication of the Calvin College archives department.

The tradition continued into the early 1960s in some parts of West Michigan, says Calvin archivist Richard Harms. He could not play Sunday ball or watch it on TV growing up in Grand Rapids and Cutlerville.

The policy posed a problem for semi-pro players because Sunday games attracted the largest crowds and paid them the most money, Harms notes.

"I remember talking to one fellow, a very good pitcher, who told me some guys would play on Sunday under a different name," recalls Harms, who has written about semi-pro leagues in West Michigan.

Vander Meer resorted to no such subterfuge. He never played semi-pro ball on Sundays for his Midland Park team, he wrote in a 1990 letter to Calvin faculty member John Bratt. "I turned down more money for a Sunday afternoon than I made all week, and I played six days a week," he wrote with some pride.

But once he signed his first contract for minor-league ball, Vander Meer wrote, "I felt ... if anyone had an outstanding talent in a trade, that was good, and it was a sin not to use it."

His sister noted his manager at Cincinnati, Bill McKechnie, let Vander Meer miss Sunday game warm-ups so he could attend church. He always did, she says.

"We know what he stood for, but a lot of the church people didn't," said Nywening, who still attends Midland Park CRC.

Despite Vander Meer's desire to pitch on Sundays and still raise his family in the church, the leaders of Midland Park CRC insisted he could not do both. He joined another denomination that did not oppose Sunday ball but never spoke ill of the church that did, his sister says.

"I'm very proud of my Dutch heritage, my association and background in the Christian Reformed Church," he wrote prior to his death in 1997.

Today, his church is proud of him, says the Rev. Peter Hoytema of Midland Park CRC. He notes the town library has a display honoring Vander Meer, including two baseballs he threw in the no-hitters.

"People speak kind of proudly of it, and the local connection we have to this record which probably will never be broken," Hoytema said.

He adds that the church should do something to honor Vander Meer on the 70th anniversary of his unique feat.

"Back in 1938, you probably would have had some elders angry at you for doing that," he says with a chuckle. "But I think next year it should be fine."

July 7, 2007

Hank Greenberg's ghost still haunts me

As a boy going to baseball games with my father at Tiger Stadium, I was in awe of Hank Greenberg's ghost.

I could envision the mighty Detroit slugger of the 1930s stepping to the plate and hammering a line drive straight into the centerfield scoreboard. That's how far Dad said Greenberg could wallop a home run back in those days.

I grew up worshipping Greenberg, along with Charlie Gehringer, Schoolboy Rowe and others my dad cheered on the 1935 championship team. Those historic Tigers ran like black-and-white ghosts across the fields of my boyhood, flickering ancestors of my own heroes: Kaline, Horton et al.

I didn't know then what hell Greenberg endured as Major League Baseball's first Jewish star. I did not even know he was Jewish, nor would I have cared if I did. All I cared about was that Hankus Pankus, as fans called him, hit 58 home runs one year and drove in 183 another.

The reality of Greenberg's life, and of America at that time, was much harder. Although not the first Jew to play big-league ball, Greenberg smashed the faith barrier a decade before Jackie Robinson broke the color barrier in 1947.

Robinson's achievement is celebrated in the new movie "42," released this week. Greenberg's less legendary feat is lauded in "Hank Greenberg: The Hero of Heroes" by John Rosengren, recently published by New American Library.

As a new season gets underway, the book is a timely reminder of the game's role in leveling the playing field of American life – and of how virulent religious prejudice was not that long ago.

As its title suggests, Rosengren's book does not understate Greenberg's accomplishments. But the ample biography brings forth the appalling racist invective Greenberg endured and the widespread anti-Semitism of his era – with luminaries such as auto icon Henry Ford leading the charge.

Ford's weekly newspaper, the Dearborn Independent, blamed Jews for subverting Christianity and capitalism and for the infamous 1919 "Black Sox" scandal in which the Chicago team threw the World Series. "The Peril of Baseball – Too Much Jew," his paper proclaimed.

The Ku Klux Klan thrived in Detroit along with a black-hooded offshoot called the Black Legion, which plotted to poison milk in Jewish neighborhoods. Meanwhile, opposing players rode Greenberg mercilessly, calling him "kike" and "Moe" (short for Moses).

Rosengren also lovingly describes the devotion of American Jews to a man who overcame harassment and flat feet to become not just a baseball star, but an inspiration to his people.

"How did Greenberg do today?" Jewish parents asked their kids who had listened to the game on the radio, Rosengren writes. Immigrants may not have known much about baseball, but they sure knew about Hank Greenberg.

"Through his own assimilation, Greenberg facilitated the assimilation of the generation that preceded him," Rosengren writes. "Greenberg became important to them because he helped them understand America through baseball."

America also came to understand more about Judaism thanks to Greenberg. Rosengren describes in detail Greenberg's difficult decision to play on Rosh Hashanah, the Jewish New Year, during the 1934 pennant race. He had promised his parents he wouldn't play on the High Holy Days but did not want to let his team down.

He played and hit two home runs to win the game. When he attended services the next morning for Rosh Hashanah's second day, members of Congregation Shaarey Zedek applauded him. One Jewish historian calls it "an iconic moment in American Jewish history."

Eight days later, with the pennant more assured, Greenberg did not play on Yom Kippur, the Day of Atonement. Detroit poet Edgar A. Guest lauded him for holding "to his teaching and the old tradition true," 31 years before Sandy Koufax more famously sat out the first game of the 1965 World Series for Yom Kippur.

Today, the Judaism of such stars as Ryan Braun and Kevin Youkilis is not widely remarked upon. Nor would racist razzing be tolerated in the age of cell-phone cameras and instant media, says Jason Miller, a conservative rabbi and Tigers fan from Farmington Hills.

"These days if a fan yelled out an anti-Semitic slur when Youkilis came to bat, it would be on (ESPN) SportsCenter 20 minutes later," says Miller, who writes about sports and other issues on his blog, rabbijason.com.

As for Greenberg's Rosh Hashanah decision, Miller says it was more symbolic than religious. Playing ball on Jewish holidays is no different from playing on Saturday, the Jewish Sabbath, which ballplayers and other athletes do routinely, he says.

"There are enough Jewish role models for children that we don't need to put professional ballplayers on a pedestal once a year on Yom Kippur," Miller says.

Greenberg still looms large in Jewish lore, says Miller, who is on the planning board of the Hank Greenberg Memorial Golf Invitational. He loves taking his family to Comerica Park and seeing Tigers like Miguel Cabrera and Victor Martinez, stars of another immigrant group assimilating into America with help from a great game.

"It's just remarkable," Miller says. "You look around, and it's such a great cross-section of Americana."

The picture is a long ways from perfect. But thanks to brave men like Greenberg and Robinson, it's a lot better than it was.

April 8, 2013

Then God said, 'Batter up!'

"*S*ix days you shall labor, and do all your work; but the *seventh day is a Sabbath to the LORD your God; in it you shall not do any work ... but only sit back and enjoy a double-header." – God*

I admit I made up that last part. But I do think God wants us to enjoy baseball on the Sabbath.

Let me rephrase that: I think God created baseball to be a Sabbath. Surely, there is no more restful, less stressful way to spend three hours than watching baseball.

The sleepy, familiar rhythms of baseball are a tonic to the harried soul and a gift from above. If Sabbath-keeping is about doing no work, reviving the spirit and giving it all to God, baseball qualifies.

God looked down at Adam swatting a rock with a stick, and saw that it was good. And He said, "But there must be a pitcher, and 90 feet between bases." Thus Nolan Ryan was born in God's mind.

Forgive my poetic excesses here. Having just returned from a week in heaven — also known as Lakeland, Fla., spring training home to the Detroit Tigers — my heart is filled with the soul-nurturing gifts of the great game.

It was a week spent with my dad, who imparted these gifts to me as a young boy. Baseball is the strong thread of our lifelong friendship, pulling us through arguments over the Beatle haircut and that big dent in the front fender.

Dad is the only guy I know who is as overjoyed as I am to watch five baseball games in five days, games where the score doesn't even matter. So we did.

So did a bunch of other geezers, young and old. Some came on canes and walkers. They are the kind lovingly described by Roger Angell, the Psalmist of baseball Scripture.

"Their loyalty to the home club is gentle and unquestioning, and their afternoon pleasure appears scarcely affected by victory or defeat," Angell wrote in 1962.

Nothing much has changed in 40 years, except the players and hot dogs cost a lot more. The wieners, too, I believe, were part of God's plan for baseball.

Ever notice how no one ever agrees on who invented baseball? No, it wasn't Doubleday, they say. No, it didn't come from rounders, they say. Some guys just started playing it in the Civil War. The reason no one knows is because God did it.

And then God said, "There must be nine innings and nine players. The best player shall be called shortstop. Don't ask me why. And in a span of 1,000 years shall come a chosen shortstop, and he shall be called Jeter."

If you haven't experienced the nirvana of Joker Marchant Stadium, ringed with palms along a busy Lakeland drag, I can't really convey it. Let's just say it's a place where you can stand by the field, baseball in hand, waiting for a player to come by and sign it. In the meantime, you chat with whoever's next to you, knowing they are a baseball soul mate.

"So, who signed your ball?" I asked the 8- or 9-year-old boy next to me. "Let's see," he said, turning it over to reveal a neat signature. "I got this one from Alan Trammel. Is he a coach or somethin'?"

In the same country as Marchant Stadium lies a place called Historic Bok Sanctuary. It was created in 1922 by Edward Bok who, being Dutch, worked his tail off to make a garden paradise on Earth. In the center of its 1,000 plants is a 205-foot bell tower.

Bok lived by his grandmother's words: "Make the world a bit better or more beautiful because you have lived in it."

I stood in the gardens, orange blossom perfume surrounding me, while the bell tower played "How Great Thou Art." Indeed.

If we are to live our faith more than one day a week, we must keep the Sabbath faithfully as well. We must find Sabbath times to relieve the grinding stress of making the world a bit better.

Dad and I needed Sabbath, and found it in Lakeland. Thirty years separate us, but baseball bonds us. The Tigers won only one game. Dad and I won it all, and didn't even have to throw a pitch.

And then God said, "There must be an ump, and he shall wear blue. Four balls are a walk, three strikes and you shall be out. Balks, I'll figure those out later.

"OK then, let's play ball!"

March 27, 2004

Third Inning

Leading the Way

'God has brought me this far'

Ed Dobson is on the podium, preaching the gospel as only he can.

Dressed in a gray cardigan and loafers, he's preaching to Mars Hill Bible Church on the first Sunday of Advent. His son, Kent, Mars Hill's pastor, listens as his father speaks of the comfort that Scripture, his wife and family give him in times of despair.

"I find my greatest hope comes from the people around me," says Dobson, who's surrounded by thousands right now.

Then he takes a seat in an easy chair at the corner of the stage. He tells Kent, "I'm going to sit down and go to sleep. So if you want me to say something, wake me up."

Without missing a beat, Kent replies, "Well, I went to sleep in many of your sermons."

The Mars Hills crowd roars with laughter. This Abbott-and-Costello bit comes amid a father-son preaching lesson at the church where Kent this fall was named pastor. They make a great tag team, Kent preaching with the biblical insight and restless energy his dad displayed in his 18 years at Calvary Church, Ed interjecting plain-spoken wisdom.

But the comic moment doesn't disguise the hard reality that everyone in the room realizes: Ed Dobson has ALS, and one day it will take his life.

It has been a dozen years since Dobson was diagnosed with ALS, or Lou Gehrig's disease, which generally claims people within two to five years. Why Dobson has survived so much longer is as much a mystery as why he got it in the first place.

But his survival is a mixed blessing. As he tells the Mars Hill crowd, his arms don't work well. His wife, Lorna, helps feed and dress him. His breath is shorter and he speaks more slowly than he used to.

That may be so, but what I hear from Dobson this morning reflects the strength and unwavering faith he's exemplified from the day I met him nearly 20 years ago. Picking up on Kent's Advent theme of hopeful expectation, Ed admits that silently waiting on God is a struggle for him.

"I spent most of my life working hard at helping people rearrange the furniture in their lives," says Dobson, who retired from Calvary in 2005. "But now, I have no agenda. I am weak. And waiting on the Lord is a challenge. A lot easier to say 'get ready' than it is to wait on the Lord.

"But this one thing I know: God has brought me this far," he says, his voice quavering slightly. "The God who brought me this far will deal with today and tomorrow. So I can rest in his coming into my life to rearrange my furniture."

He sits back in his easy chair, and the congregation sings "Come, Thou Long-Expected Jesus."

A few days later, he's sitting on the couch of his and Lorna's Kentwood condominium. Out the window they admire three deer grazing around the ravine of Plaster Creek. Their airy two-level is filled with photos of their grandchildren, framed biblical quotes and the aroma of Lorna's baking shortbread.

Always wiry, Ed's frame has been thinned by ALS. He was a star soccer player growing up in Northern Ireland. A coach at Liberty University, where Dobson was an administrator, once told him he could have turned pro. As a man of deep faith, Ed Dobson believes God could heal him of ALS. So, I ask, why do you think God hasn't done that?

"There is no good answer, so I've never asked it," he replies. Adds Lorna, "If you're always obsessed about having to have answers, you can't really live."

But Dobson grapples with the question in his book, "Seeing Through the Fog: Hope When Your World Falls Apart." In its 145 pages, which he dictated by voice to his computer, he recounts his journey with ALS from the moment he first felt a twitching in his eyelid on his 50th birthday. Nearly a year later, just before Thanksgiving 2000, a University of Michigan doctor told him he had probable ALS.

As Lorna drove him back to Grand Rapids, he writes, "I felt like my life was over. I felt like I had been buried alive."

With such unstinting detail, Dobson traces the painful path he has walked since, as well as scenes from his life before ALS. Through it all, with Lorna ever at his side, he's held fast to faith and "a hope that comes with strength: the strength to keep living life, despite its challenges, and to continually give thanks for the blessings we have, even in the darkest of times."

It's easy to lose hope when he thinks about his future, Dobson says. So he thinks about today, counsels other ALS patients and watches "The Three Stooges" to make sure he laughs. When he gets down, he repeats God's assurance from Hebrews: "Never will I leave you; never will I forsake you."

Most of all, he gives thanks for the many blessings he still has — especially Lorna, their children Kent, Daniel and Heather, and their six grandchildren. Soon they all will gather for the holidays.

After he was diagnosed 12 years ago, Dobson thought that Christmas would be his last. This year, he looks forward to another one – and hopes for many more.

Dec. 11, 2012

Brother's love, pastor's forgiveness

When the Rev. Charlie Jones was about 12, he and his older brother Willie were walking along a Mississippi back road when four teenage boys rode up on horses.

The white teens tried to run the two black youths over, forcing Charlie and Willie to jump into a ditch. When the riders came after them, Willie and Charlie fought back.

This was in the 1940s, when black boys and men didn't always return home from a fight like that. Charlie and Willie were saved by a white man who drove up, scared the white teens off and later defended the Jones boys in front of the farmer they worked for.

Charlie Jones says he thought of that fight after learning Willie had been brutally murdered by four Kent County young men who abducted him from a bowling alley parking lot.

"If I could have been there at the parking lot, things would have been different," Jones recalls telling Kent County Prosecutor William Forsyth.

But Jones let go of that thought. He had to, just as he had to let go of any hatred he might have felt toward those who killed his beloved brother and only sibling.

"I hold on to some memories, but the grief you don't have to hold on to," Jones says. "Then you are able to forgive people."

We are sitting in the basement office of his Southeast Grand Rapids church, Macedonia Missionary Baptist. On the wall behind him is a photo of him and Willie in white suits and smiles, taken when they sang in a traveling gospel group in the 1950s and '60s.

Pastor Jones is speaking in remarkably tranquil tones about the horrific beating, kidnapping and robbery of his 66-year-old brother last March. Willie Jones was left to die in the woods from multiple stab wounds and blows to his head and body.

Last month, three of his abductors were convicted of murder, and a fourth pleaded guilty to second-degree murder.

Just reading about this evil killing sickens me. Charlie Jones refuses to entertain bitterness or dwell on what he cannot change.

"There is no way to make my brother come back," he says in a gentle voice. "There's no use holding onto that and allowing myself to be reduced to hatred."

Sometimes a man's memory is best served by the way his loved ones honor him. Willie Jones' death was tragic, but he would be honored indeed to see how his family and friends have handled it.

During the trial, the Rev. Jones and others reached out to the families of the convicted men with astonishing compassion. They listened sympathetically and wrapped their arms around one youth's mother. Pastor Jones tried to comfort a mother grieving that she would lose her son to prison.

"If I can't forgive people, then God is not going to forgive me if I trespass against somebody," reasons Jones, 65. Willie would have agreed, he adds.

"'You just have to forgive folks and go on' — that's all he would say."

Charlie and Willie learned forgiveness in the unforgiving life of a Mississippi sharecropper's family. Raised mostly by their grandmother, they worked in the cotton fields around Tupelo.

No matter how hard they worked they were usually in debt to the landowners, and got little more than clothes at Christmas.

The boys stuck close together through hateful times. On one farm, they saw their house burn down in a fire set by the landowner's son. Young Charlie once saw a man hanged after being accused of stealing from a store clerk.

But the boys also saw small kindnesses, such as one landowner who allowed them to take his truck to town on Saturday nights. In church and from his grandmother, Charlie learned not to return hatred with hatred, a lesson he passed on to his children.

He sticks to his nonviolent philosophy now, when others might cry for vengeance. He has seen his loving attitude come back to him, with hugs and grateful whispers wherever he goes.

But make no mistake — Pastor Jones hurts. Whenever Willie came to his church, the Rev. Jones would step out of the pulpit and proudly announce, "This is my brother, y'all!"

If Willie were alive now, over the holidays, "We'd have been together, laughing and talking," he adds.

He can't afford to dwell on that.

As Willie said, you just have to forgive folks and go on.

Dec. 2, 2000

The mysterious joy of sisterhood

Mary Fabbro stands smiling in the sun, hands set brashly on hips, basking in the joy of being 17 with the whole world before her.

It's a golden moment from the summer of 1946, when Mary was staying at the lakeside cottage of her friend, Dolores Schroeder.

That fall, she entered the doors of Marywood convent to become a nun.

"The day I entered, my dad drove me across town," recalls the woman now named Sister Amata. "I cried the whole way. He said, 'I'll take you home.' I said, 'No, Dad, I have to go.'"

Her homesick heart ached that day, when she left her close Italian family, and a young man who wanted to marry her, to enter the order of Dominican sisters.

But today Sister Amata smiles as joyfully as that 17-year-old when she looks back on her life of service to God. If she had the chance, she'd do it again.

"I have found such joy and satisfaction in my life," says Sister Amata, bubbling with memories and laughter at her Aquinas College office. "I feel just awful about it sometimes. I think, how do I deserve all this?"

People like Sister Amata deserve all this and more.

Dolores Schroeder was among the friends honoring her in a celebration of her 50th anniversary as a Dominican at Our Lady of Sorrows Church, the little Italian parish where young Mary Fabbro grew up.

One of four children of Andrew and Margaret Fabbro, she disliked school until she came in the fourth grade to Our Lady, staffed by Dominican sisters. She loved nuns like Sister Conrad and tiny Sister Samuel.

"I just thought she came from heaven every day, because she was so pretty and nice," recalls Sister Amata, her curly brown hair framing a lively, delicate face. "One day I looked down and saw she had feet. I nearly died."

The sisters confirmed her desire to become a nun. "I thought it was the way I could be closer to God — that was my whole idea," she says, laughing at her childish simplicity. But then she adds, "After all, what are we here for? To make our way back to God."

But as she attended high school at Marywood Academy, other possibilities beckoned. Dick Lindsay offered one. He hung around Loveland's Drug Store, where Mary worked, sipping soda water until it closed. One day, he proposed. Sister Amata recreates the moment with drama.

"I said, 'Oh, Dick, I'm going to be a sister.' He was just horrified. I felt terrible, just terrible."

He went to war and wrote her letters from the South Pacific. He died a couple of Christmases ago.

"I'm glad I went through that," she says. "You know what it is to give up that kind of love, which is a wonderful love. But it wasn't for me.

"This is my way," clasping her hands over her heart. "I don't know how to explain it. It's the mystery of the religious vocation."

The mystery led her to hallowed Marywood. She was received as a novice in the spring of 1947 — the starting point of her anniversary — and a year later took vows of poverty, chastity and obedience. She took the name Amata, Latin for "the loved one."

She found a rich life in sisterhood, a life of simplicity, deep spiritual growth, a caring community and a rewarding career. She taught at several Catholic schools before coming to Aquinas 30 years ago, where she chairs the theology department and teaches Scripture.

How has sisterhood changed in 50 years? "Well, look," she says, tugging at her pink dress, a far cry from the long habit she once wore. The day she took off her veil, she went to the mall and bought an ice cream cone.

Dominicans are more open to the world, socially active and religiously ecumenical. They've also fallen from more than 700 women to about 350, declining drastically like all religious orders. But Sister Amata suspects there's a divine design at work.

"I think we could be going through a dead-ash time, and we're going to revitalize," she says. "Or maybe religious life is going to take a different turn. I never put anything past that Holy Spirit.

"I wish young women could realize what they're missing, what true joy they're missing."

Sister Amata hasn't missed joy. She has lived close to God, gladly offering him her celibate love.

Besides, she says, "I would have driven a man nuts. Oh, I'm a horrible cook."

July 12, 1997

Dalai Lama: be kind, giggle often

Before he launched into a four-hour presentation on basic Buddhism, the Dalai Lama confessed he would only tackle the easier parts of the ancient text he was about to discuss.

"To try to go word by word, I need some homework," the Tibetan holy man said. "I'm lazy to carry that homework."

His Holiness' humble line got a big laugh from the crowd of 7,300 at Ann Arbor's Crisler Arena. So did several other remarks he made after entering the arena, bowing with folded hands as the crowd rose to greet him in reverent silence.

But once the Dalai Lama began his two-part lecture on wisdom and compassion, he became the master teacher and we his students. Monks seated lotus-style around him, actor Richard Gere took notes in the front row and spiritual pilgrims from West Michigan listened to teachings ranging from disarmingly simple to nearly impenetrable.

"At the root of all our suffering lies a form of ignorance, a form of unknowing," he said in Tibetan through an interpreter, switching from the English with which he greeted the audience.

That was clear enough, as were his "antidotes" for removing ignorance. Wagging his finger, he told of the Four Noble Truths, the three turnings of the wheel of Dharma, the two types of suffering — a system for eliminating misery and helping others.

But after Buddhism 101 in the morning, the 72-year-old monk taught a post-lunch graduate course on the nature of the self. It's safe to say many of us failed, this religion reporter included.

A thinned-out crowd bravely tried to follow his esoteric discussion of whether the self is separate from the mind and body, or even has a beginning.

"The ultimate awakening mind is the wisdom that directly realizes emptiness," he said at one point. Wow. I just wanted to know how to stop worrying so much.

Still, there was palpable power in seeing a Nobel Prize winner and global spiritual leader gently set foot in our part of the universe. Those who traveled two hours from Grand Rapids were not disappointed.

"It just reminded me how great of a teacher he is," said Brian Bowe, 36, a communications specialist at Grand Valley State University. "I could be working on this the rest of my life, and there's so much more."

For Heidi Ragchaa of Walker, a former Protestant, it was an "amazing" opportunity to see a spiritual and political powerhouse with a delightful giggle. For her husband, Adiya, it was reconnecting with a man he met several times when he was a monk in Mongolia and India.

"I believed in him ever since I was a kid," said Adiya, 27. "Everywhere he goes he teaches about compassion, love, peace."

But despite abstaining from political talk, His Holiness could not escape the whirlwind surrounding his struggle for autonomy in Tibet. Well over 100 Chinese protesters lined the gate in front of the arena, insisting China rightfully rules Tibet and freed it from a cruel feudal system.

For Tenzin Bhagen, a Tibetan whose father was killed by the Chinese after they invaded in 1951, the sight brought back painful memories. He escaped from Tibet by walking across the Himalayas, eventually earning a degree from GVSU in 2004.

"It was the same thing I saw as a child during the (Chinese) Cultural Revolution," said Bhagen, 42, a Washington, D.C., resident who leads tours of Tibet.

Seeing the Dalai Lama calmed him down, but he regretted his fellow Tibetans can't hear the message of peace and cooperation.

"All these people have the opportunity to see him, while the people in Tibet are just dying to see him," he said.

Those who came to Ann Arbor were greeted with metal detectors and exotic pageantry. Vendors sold colorful shawls and beads, while maroon-robed monks roamed the halls. A beautiful sand painting was displayed in front of a showcase of University of Michigan basketball stars' jerseys.

Inside, the Dalai Lama's platform was richly arrayed with images of the Buddha and his teachers, a table of fruit and bread and an intricately carved sculpture made of butter.

His Holiness cheerfully exhorted us to follow our own religious traditions, saying fundamentalists of all faiths spread fear and division.

"Under such circumstances, efforts to promote genuine harmony on the basis of mutual understanding, mutual respect of different traditions, is very, very essential," he said.

That's a key teaching of this smiling little monk. But so is his call to see reality for what it is. How many of us know the reality of Tibet's history? How many will follow the patient practices he prescribes?

Achieving peace is hard, whether inside yourself or in the world. The message I got from His Holiness was this: be kind, be disciplined, and do your homework.

April 20, 2008

Duncan, Les and a fracas of friends

Lester DeKoster and Duncan Littlefair are going at each other with a vengeance, and loving every minute of it.

Nose to nose, hunched forward, they're arguing theology at the corner table of their favorite restaurant. Each week, they gather here, along with the Rev. John deWitt, to hash out their gaping philosophical differences — and to share the rarest of friendships.

I'm here as a guest of this most distinguished group, which produces possibly the most delectable discourse on religion in all Grand Rapids. Fairly intimidated, I try to keep my head down except to occasionally feed them more morsels to chew over.

At the moment, the fiercely independent Littlefair is taking DeKoster and deWitt to task for their habit of quoting Scripture and scholars to bolster their arguments.

"You people are submissive!" thunders Littlefair. "You're always quoting! Who cares what (John) Calvin said? ... It's your authority, not theirs!"

"That is arrogant," retorts DeKoster, as gentle-mannered and steel-willed as Littlefair is hard-eyed and soft-hearted. "When Calvin says 'the Bible says,' boy, I believe it."

But it doesn't take long before their face-off melts into laughter, which is the warm music of this lunchtime theological slugfest — or perhaps I should call it intellectual racquetball.

It is a delight to watch. While others yell insults at their ideological enemies, these men argue with laughter and love.

A more unlikely matchup would be hard to imagine: Littlefair, 83, the feisty free-thinker who preached for decades at ultra-liberal Fountain Street Church, vs. arch-conservatives DeKoster, 80, the retired fire-breathing editor of the Christian Reformed Banner, and deWitt, 59, whose Seventh Reformed Church's policy protests got it expelled from the denomination. Sometimes the Rev. Richard Rhem from liberal Christ Community Church comes and balances the scorecard.

What they share is a rebellious independence of thought and a passion for religion. They're drawn together by a love of ideas, a taste for debate and a deep friendship. That friendship, says deWitt, is based on "regard, respect and affection," not ideological agreement. "People don't understand how you can care for someone with whom you do not agree."

In fact, says DeKoster, their deeply held convictions give them the confidence to tangle as friends: "You can extend your hand with the utmost sincerity when you know who you are."

As a model of constructive disagreement, religious or otherwise, I don't think you can beat this weekly fracas of friends. In a country where warring political and religious factions are firing salvos of judgment at each other, these guys show you can disagree with delight and goodwill.

DeKoster and Littlefair have been holding their weekly lunch ritual for about four years, the last two with deWitt. They clearly like each other, and clearly love to argue.

If you visit this modern-day Algonquin roundtable, however, be prepared to duck. The ideas fly fast and furious, from Luther to liberalism to salvation. Quotes from Augustine and Santayana mingle with references to Rush Limbaugh and the Quebec referendum. Theological repartee doesn't get much better than this.

"Anybody who assumes that God can be found only through Christianity has got to be living in another age," blusters Littlefair.

"'No man cometh unto the father but by me,'" quotes DeKoster, amused and avuncular in his tweed coat. "We have no problem with that."

"That's your problem you don't have a problem with that," grumbles Littlefair.

DeWitt stays mainly out of the fray, but offers this praise: "I've never had a more probing, intelligent critic than Duncan." Adds Littlefair, "You get a better hearing from this outrageous naturalist than you do from your own (denomination)."

Between the banter, Littlefair advises deWitt to take time out from his job for rest and reflection, and deWitt asks about Littlefair's dog. When Littlefair makes the mistake of praising the "genius of Christianity," DeKoster pounces with twinkling eyes. "You don't think that's a senile fallback into your childhood?" he needles.

"It doesn't bother me one damn bit," Littlefair insists, then breaks into helpless laughter with his friends. "Come and challenge me," he says, raising a toast. "Ah, Les . . ."

Nov. 18, 1995

Berrigan a humble prophet of justice

"Here, let's just open these and see if they fit," the young pharmacist said, cracking open a packet of tiny batteries.

The Rev. Daniel Berrigan was clearly pleased with her helpfulness, as was I. We were in Fulton Heights Foods on a modest mission: to find Father Berrigan a toothbrush and a battery for his hearing aid.

At the conclusion of our interview at the Dominican Center at Marywood, he'd asked me if I could drive him somewhere to find them.

As if I'm going to say, "Sorry, Father, I'm kinda busy right now." The man is a legend to me. A lift to the grocery was not a problem.

So I found myself searching the aisles of Fulton Heights Foods with the man who's made a life of promoting peace, who burned draft cards back in 1968 when I was prime fodder for Vietnam.

In his flannel shirt and corduroys, this 76-year-old, smallish man with thinning hair attracted zero attention. The helpful pharmacist could not have known she was helping a famous Jesuit priest who was spending two weeks lecturing and mingling at Aquinas College.

I felt a twinge of West Michigan pride as the woman, with a Ferris State pin on her white coat, sorted through the batteries to find the right one for Berrigan. He thanked her warmly, noting he would never have gotten such help in New York City. Then I helped him pick out a toothbrush, since he'd forgotten his.

Besides the egotistical honor of being able to help this man in any way, our little sojourn brought home to me the obvious: The guy's just a human being.

Not a profound thought, but one easily overlooked in the culture of celebrity. Berrigan is really an anti-celebrity, whose life of grassroots political action, writing and study has nothing to do with fame and everything to do with justice. Yet I still fancy him a celebrity, a larger-than-life hero.

So what's wrong with heroism? What's wrong is when we idolize the person and ignore what he or she stands for.

Berrigan talked about this when our conversation touched on the deaths of Mother Teresa and Princess Diana.

He had "great admiration" for Mother Teresa but disagreed with her lack of concern with the causes of poverty. He admitted to having little interest in Princess Diana before she died, and only then learned of her admirable efforts to ban land mines and help the suffering.

Berrigan sympathized with the outpouring of grief and donations to charity occasioned by Diana's death. But he invoked the name of another anti-hero, the Catholic social reformer Dorothy Day, to illustrate the perils of idolization.

"She would say in her salty fashion, 'Don't call me a saint — that's too easy,'" Berrigan said in his thoughtful fashion." If people have other people on pedestals, they can walk away. They've made their bow.

"Let's all try to be human together. Learn something from good people — but walk with it."

In other words, pressure President Clinton to sign an international treaty banning land mines. Look beyond Mother Teresa's death to the impoverished people she worked with. And don't just admire Father Berrigan — listen to him.

Berrigan's message remains undiminished. He's not an icon of the '60s protest movement. He's a prophet of injustice today.

"There's more misery, more war, more racism," Berrigan asserted. "There's war domestically against the poor. War has become a much more virulent metaphor for an assault on human beings."

Ask him about the Catholic Church's response to injustice, and Berrigan struggles to answer. Then he says, "It's at the bottom that the real things are going on." The Grand Rapids Dominican sisters, he says, are "a very exciting example of what can be done, very quietly."

In Berrigan's theo-political world view, the Sermon on the Mount is a call for political clout for the masses: "Christ is blessing those at the bottom and promising them new power."

It's down there, among the poor in spirit, the meek and mourning and hungry, that Berrigan sees change happening. Not the people of People magazine, but the people of the streets of London and Calcutta. People like us.

Daniel Berrigan is not like me. But I do him a disservice to put him on a pedestal. He is deeply human, which is why he does what he does.

As I dropped him off after our shopping trip, he said, "Don't forget my epitaph: 'It was never dull.'"

Somehow, I think we'll say more than that.

Sept. 20, 1997

Rabbi Al and Shirley: the music of love

Rabbi Al Lewis set the cello on a stand in his living room, an elegant testimony to his love of music and the woman who gave it to him.

Shirley Lewis gave Al the handsome instrument in 1978. He took some lessons, but then got busy as a rabbi. After 30 years of loaning it out, he is finally getting around to playing it.

Luckily, Shirley, an accomplished musician, is there to tune it for him.

This is how things go in a marriage of 45 years. Husband and wife balance each other. They help each other through success, stress and sickness. And, if they see it through, one finally learns the cello.

The Lewises celebrate each day of seeing it through.

Their friends joined them in joy with an anniversary dinner at Temple Emanuel, the congregation Rabbi Lewis served for 28 years before retiring in 2000.

For Al and Shirley, it was a moving affirmation of love surviving suffering.

"It was saying, 'We've been through it; we've come out the other side, and we are celebrating,'" recalls Al, who turns 67 soon. "It's spring again. We believe every day is a blessing."

The Lewises weathered a tough winter, metaphorically and literally.

So do many couples blessed with lifelong relationships. Thank goodness for the love, because the aging can be brutal.

Shirley, 66, was an emergency-room regular last year. Complications from diabetes paralyzed her stomach, drastically slowing her digestion. Pneumonia hospitalized her over the holidays. And, in October, Al came home to find her laid out with insulin shock.

"Had he not come home when he did, I would not be here," Shirley says.

All this compounded other health problems that forced her to retire in 2004 from Aquinas College, where she was dean of arts and sciences and twice named outstanding faculty member. Aquinas honored her and Al with its Emeritus Award. Al is former director of the Emeritus College.

That and the anniversary dinner the next night were "the two most affirming days of my life," Shirley says. She cried for a day afterward, sensing "the fragility of life, and how incredibly wonderful it is sometimes."

Right now, she's enjoying the wonderful.

"These times are very sweet, very gentle, when we're both well," she says. "You know that it's going to end at some point."

She and Al know well the spirituality of mortality. They co-teach an Aquinas course on death and dying. Al was the founding president of Hospice of West Michigan and has taught and written on the aging process along with his thoughtful columns in The Press.

But living through the physical and emotional stuff life throws at the most loving of couples is no small challenge.

They meet it the best they can each day, nurtured by their community, faith and family. They cook together and savor every moment with grandchildren Max, Ellie and Jacob. Shirley prays often, holding "long conversations with God."

Oh, yes, and music. She has gotten back to piano while Al learns the cello. They both have time now. And every day is a blessing.

"I'm here for you, and you're here for me, and the rest falls in place," he tells her.

The light pours into their living room, sweet and gentle.

May 30, 2009

Tutu smiles in the face of evil

Archbishop Desmond Tutu is a little guy. You would look right over his head in a crowded room. But you wouldn't miss him, because he would be the one everyone was listening to.

This small, soft-voiced man filled the entirety of Van Andel Arena Tuesday night. About 6,000 people listened as he told tales of tortured Africans, some too depraved to repeat here. He heard those stories as chairman of South Africa's Truth and Reconciliation Commission, which granted amnesty to many who confessed to the evils they committed under apartheid.

Then Tutu smiled.

"Yes, each one of us has this extraordinary capacity for evil," Tutu said in his lecture sponsored by the World Affairs Council of West Michigan.

If any of us grew up in the same environment, perhaps we would have done equally evil things, Tutu said.

So then, what was he smiling about?

"Yes, we have this capacity for evil," he repeated. "But remarkably, gloriously, we have a capacity for good. It is quite extraordinary. We are fundamentally good!"

Coming from the person sitting next to you at worship, this statement would be encouraging but hardly surprising.

Coming from Tutu, it is a revelation of the human spirit.

This man sat through horror story upon horror story, hearing the worst of which people are capable. He heard men in suits admit to burning black activists, or drugging 10 of them and blowing them up in a minibus — stories that shocked people across South Africa.

On this Tuesday night, Tutu turned shock into grace, torture into transcendence.

If a country capable of such horrors can be reformed nonvio-
lently, he told us, then no place on earth is beyond redemption.

For me, the message went deeper. If Desmond Tutu can live
under hate's yoke for most of his life, and smilingly proclaim
people to be basically good, I have to believe he's got something
there.

He makes you believe with his meekness and his devilish
humor. He does not rail against violence, he sweet-talks you out
of it. With the gentlest of laughs, he points you toward your best
self, and God.

"We are an incredible paradox," he said. "We are infinite crea-
tures created for the infinite." He quoted St. Augustine: "Our
souls are restless until they rest in thee."

It's no mystery he was awarded the 1984 Nobel Peace Prize,
though it is a wonder he wasn't murdered before he helped over-
turn the torturers. Tutu's persuasive powers brought to the arena Christians, Jews, Muslims and no particular believers, politi-
cians, preachers and protesters.

Some hoped for a strong anti-war statement, which Tutu has
not been shy about making in interviews and protest events.
Perhaps he refrained because lives are being lost or he chose to
be pastoral to our religious region. He touched on the war only
when asked and then, ever so gently, asked why a "great country" that helped free his land would tarnish its proud legacy.

He spoke of opening an Ebony magazine at age 9 and being
inspired by a photo of Jackie Robinson. He thanked us, again
and again, for the protests, prayers and political acts that
helped him experience Robinson's freedom.

He didn't rail at us. He shamed us by reminding us how good
we really are.

Perhaps the night's most surprising moment was when a student asked him the biggest obstacle he has overcome.

Well, duh, it's apartheid, I thought.

Tutu said it was always having to be the man white South
Africans hated, always having to denounce people when he just
wanted to be loved.

"There are times I felt, 'Why don't I shut up?' And I couldn't
do it. Because when God grabs you be the scruff of the neck,
you've had it."

He grabbed us all when he pictured God urging humanity to "soar toward the transcendent," like an eagle.

Raising his hands heavenward, he whispered, "We are those made for laughter, for joy, for goodness, for peace ... . We are made by God. We are all family, all family, all family."

The applause rose to a roar, like the beating of 6,000 eagles' wings.

March 29, 2003

Abney passes on to glory, with joy

If Bishop William Abney could have jumped up and started shouting, he would have.

All around him, glorious mayhem let loose at Bethel Pentecostal Church. The spirit had caught fire at Abney's memorial service and would not be put out.

A gospel band played furiously, people clapped their hands joyously and a woman danced ecstatically around the casket of Bethel's beloved pastor, who lay in peaceful repose.

It was entirely fitting. This was the spirit Abney ignited in his 45 years at Bethel. Now his faith family was sending him home as he would have wanted, with singing, dancing, tears and laughter.

"This is not a funeral. This is a home-going celebration," the packed house proclaimed, and so it was: a celebration of a spiritual father to his congregation and an exemplary faith leader to all of West Michigan.

A week of events honoring Abney brought into clearer focus what many of us already knew. Here was a good man of God, generous, kind, passionate for justice, a sweet singer for the Lord. We were blessed to have him for so long.

Now, at age 80, he has moved on. If you are one of his faithful, you will not question he has gone home to glory.

"This is not the end," said Bishop Ronald Young of Philadelphia, who led the celebration service. "He just graduated from this earthly life, and he graduated cum laude."

Tissues circulated as with weeping and exultation Abney's church held commencement. The holy presence was palpable as they sang softly, "Lay down the burdens you have carried, for in this sanctuary God is here, God is here ... ."

It was an especially moving moment in a night filled with them. And though an outsider, I felt a welcoming warmth I have always felt at Bethel. Whether in worship or in his office, Bishop Abney made me feel that way.

His was a gentle, smiling presence. He made you feel special, like it had been too long since he'd last seen you. His slight frame and soft voice carried surprising spiritual power. When you heard that voice burst forth in song, it knocked you back on your heels.

"I Won't Complain" was his signature song, and he never did through a host of ailments. He felt too blessed to bother. Abney conveyed that grateful spirit to all of us, while firmly pushing for the right and the just.

Every once in awhile, someone comes along who speaks the spirit of God with special clarity. Quibble about theology if you must, but the sense of grace transcends race, class and creed. Bishop Abney was such a man.

At his going-home service, speaker after speaker attested to that. They called him their spiritual father, a pastor who pulled them out of addictions and despair into lives of meaning and hope, often putting them in positions of leadership.

Shellie Cole-Mickens, head of Bethel's media ministry, said she was a "thug from the street" when Abney took her to breakfast and left a $100 tip. She almost stole it, she said to uproarious laughter.

"I would not be the woman I am today were it not for Bishop Abney," she said.

Deacon David Wilson said God sent Abney to him when his life was a wreck, calling him "an angel in a world of darkness."

Abney's family made touching remarks, his sister Mamie saying, "I wanted to be just like him." His brother Norman: "He was my inspiration to be saved." Son Andre: "Daddy taught me to get on my knees and worship God."

Six of his brothers and sisters rendered "Down by the Riverside" with delightful part singing.

His wife, Lorraine, thanked God for the care her children and grandchildren gave Abney in his final days. At his death, she said, "It was glorious when he went home with the Lord."

And so it was this week. Farewell, Bishop Abney. If you won't complain, we certainly won't either.

Feb. 3, 2007

A common man of uncommon virtue

Honesty. Decency. Generosity. Faith. Humility. Diligence.

We have heard those values echoed many times to describe a good Grand Rapids man who lived by them.

With the death of former President Gerald R. Ford, these virtues of his have been praised by everyone from President Bush and Gov. Granholm to the thousands who lined up to pay their respects to his body in repose.

They're good Midwestern values, solid as a well-built front porch and familiar as Sunday dinner grace. But people talked about Ford's embodiment of them as if they were something rare today.

Perhaps they are. Or perhaps the death of Jerry Ford, as so many in West Michigan call him, simply reminds us of the best values to which we aspire as individuals and a community.

As we watched the motorcade pass by and viewed the flag-draped casket and heard the stirring hymns, we thought of Ford's faithful values almost as if they were from a bygone era. In fact, they are values we try to live by every day but seldom think about.

So Ford's passing leaves us with a gentle challenge: What do we take from this that lasts?

Are faith, honesty and generosity truly the bedrock of our Midwestern culture?

If so, can we put those to better use for one another and the common good?

Ford applied the values he learned here to a distinguished congressional career and as president to a country in crisis. His firm decisions were steeped in a strong, reconciling faith, extolled by former President Jimmy Carter at Ford's funeral at Grace Episcopal Church in East Grand Rapids.

Certainly, there is no shortage of faith in West Michigan nor of problems to address, from the ailments of the public schools Ford attended to a languishing economy.

And the fact such a loving national spotlight has shone on Ford's values says a lot about what a coarse and adversarial society we have become.

But, for me, the many stories I heard of Ford's respect toward every person he met, and how he won lasting friends by helping out ordinary people, bring his legacy down to a personal level.

How can I put in motion the prayers I say at church? How can I better serve this wonderful, problematic community? How can I be a better friend, father and son?

It is not that President Ford was a saint. That is exactly the point, his admirers say. He was one of us, a regular guy who showed us what regular people can achieve.

Surely that's one reason tens of thousands stood for hours in a biting cold to pay respects at his casket at the Gerald R. Ford Museum.

It was an incredible, inspiring display of pride and patriotism. The sense of shared community focused on its most famous son was overwhelming.

"He brought a lot of honor to Grand Rapids," said West Side resident Joan VanManen. "He was always considerate of other people. That says a lot about where he came from."

Chris Patton pushed a baby buggy as his wife, Maria, bundled her year-old son in a blanket. They drove from Buchanan to honor someone Chris called "a good, honest man" and a fellow Eagle Scout.

John Dantuma, of Muskegon, said Ford helped his brother-in-law with Lou Gehrig's disease get a job.

"If you had a problem, he'd help you," he said.

The next morning, Carrie Holmes, of Saugatuck, paid her respects. She summed Ford up simply: "He was just one of the good guys. He got to Washington, but Washington didn't get to him."

Taking video later of the presidential motorcade, LeeAnn Vallone took pride in a fellow Grand Rapidian who "dreamed big" and granted a controversial pardon.

"Midwesterners aren't afraid of doing the right thing," she said.

True enough. But our heartfelt honoring of Gerald R. Ford isn't just a Midwestern thing. It's a human thing. It's about a good man whose death points us back to basic values of faith, compassion and courage.

Surely Ford would want us to apply those values, with renewed commitment, to the community that raised him so well.

Jan. 6, 2007

Fourth Inning

Make a Joyful Noise

A gift of music, compliments of God

At 96, Ola Hall has only one explanation for how she can play piano every week at Fellowship Bible Church — the Lord.

Ola Elizabeth Hall doesn't look anywhere close to 96 years old. Eighty, maybe. She could pass for 70. As we sit down in her Northeast Grand Rapids home, she lightly laughs off the compliment.

"I don't take any medicine," she volunteers. "To me, that's wonderful. I see people taking whole handfuls of pills.

"I've been a Christian for 58 years," she adds significantly. "That helps a lot, you know. I'm not under any great stress."

Plus, she's never smoked or drank, and she's gone for check-ups every six months for 20 years. But that's all secondary, Ola believes.

"I think the Lord has just given me long life," she says, wagging her finger and laughing. "He gave me my breath, and he can take it away right now."

Luckily for us, he doesn't. Ola's husband, Lawrence, jumps in with an observation about her uncanny ability to play piano by ear.

"She can just pick it out of the air, and remember it, too," says Lawrence, a mere 82. "Ola gets the music in her mind, and it's hers from then on."

That's why Ola plays piano every week at Fellowship Bible Church in Plainfield Township. Playing along with organist Gloria Osbeck, she plays hymns, accompanies soloists and does occasional duets with Lawrence.

On the occasion of Ola's birthday, Pastor Russell Osbeck thought she deserved a little recognition.

I don't think she's gotten much, judging from her embarrassment at the attention. But since I ask, she tells me how she learned to play piano.

She was born in 1902 in Indian Territory. Five years later, it became known as Oklahoma. Her father, who had set up a store there, bought a piano when Ola was 5, so her older sister Sybil could take lessons.

Outdoorsy Sybil wasn't much interested, but Ola liked plunking the keys. Eventually, she took lessons for about a year from a woman who had to take a train to town.

When Ola was 10 her family moved to Colorado, and she attended a music conservatory for maybe six months. Then her family moved back to Oklahoma. That was the extent of her musical training.

"I got a little better as I went along," she explains.

In fact, her mom sold the piano when Ola's father died, and she didn't touch a keyboard until many years later.

"I was sitting in church one day, and they needed someone to play for the children," she recalls. "I said, I think I could play 'Jesus Loves Me, This I Know.'"

She played from then on whenever someone needed her to. She played with Lawrence, her husband of 45 years, after her first husband of 30 years died of a heart attack.

Lawrence worked in jail and prison ministry for Mel Trotter Mission, and Ola was office secretary for 11 years. She often played and sang at mission services and at the Kent County Jail.

So enough history already. Let's hear her play.

Ola sits down at her well-worn Conn organ and immediately starts in. The notes roll from her fingers, a soothing gospel hymn.

"Do you play organ?" she asks me as she plays. She starts singing along in a high vibrato. She plays so effortlessly, it's like she's shooting marbles.

"Oh me," she says with a laugh when she's done. I ask her the name of the song. That throws her. "Let's see, what was the name of that? 'Something of Love.' I can't think what the name of it is now.

"You want to sing a song with me?" she asks Lawrence. "Oh — 'Shepherd of Love' — that's the name of it."

She digs out "What a Day That Will Be" from the piano bench, and she and Lawrence begin.

"There is coming a day when no heartaches shall come, no more clouds in the sky, what a day that will be, when Jesus I shall see ...

When I compliment her playing, she bats me on the arm. "Oh, you're just funnin' me," she says.

Then I get tough with her. Come on, I ask, what's your secret?

"It just comes easy, and I don't know how," she insists. "I often wonder myself: 'How can I do that?'

"I think God has given me a gift," she finally admits. "Doesn't he say he'll give all of us a gift, all of us who come to him? I don't know, I don't know. But it has to be something from outside of myself."

I'll give her the gift part, but as to where it comes from — well, who's to say? Even Ola can't. All she can do is play, and stay away from smoking and drinking.

May 9, 1998

A buoyant Beatle helps us believe

Dear, precious Paul: Why do we love you so? It must be your boyish charm, always showing up on our doorsteps with the fresh cheekiness of a first date.

No, make that your golden voice, effortlessly scaling octaves to pluck the prettiest notes from the top of the tree.

Or perhaps it's your rock 'n' roll rakishness, as you swagger smugly across the stage with your coveted Hofner bass.

It came down to this for me Wednesday night in The Palace at Auburn Hills: Paul made me smile, and laugh, and sing. I would have screamed, if only I'd been an 11-year-old girl.

As it was, I felt a grateful lump in my throat as Paul McCartney tore into "All My Loving." He put me right back in sixth grade, watching him and his fellow Beatles turn the Ed Sullivan Show into hormone heaven.

It was a thing of wonder to watch 59-year-old Sir Paul turn the Palace into a sanctuary of unmitigated joy.

We worshipped him, as we have worshipped so many guitar gods over the years. But we also celebrated the idea of Paul, our intimate relationships with his songs, and the incandescent light he ignites in us with the awesome force of the inspired, creative mind.

There is no doubt the rock stage is a kind of mass-culture altar. Fans swarm around the feet of their electric heroes with the frenzy of true believers. They raise their hands and sway their bodies with the delirium of a Pentecostal revival.

"Clapton is God," followers of legendary guitarist Eric Clapton scrawled on London subway walls in the 1960s. Eric endures, but our adulation of the guitar gods often is tragically shattered.

From Elvis to Jimi Hendrix to Kurt Cobain, their stature shrinks from hopelessly oversized icons to all-too-human shape in an instant of overindulgence or self-hatred.

With Paul, you have something different. He does not need to super-size himself. He is inherently huge, with a magnitude born of the Beatles legend and his creative genius. But he is also life-size, a likable bloke who sings of ordinary loneliness and happiness, of longing for yesterday and faith that it's getting better all the time.

Paul connects us not only with that catalog of incomparable Lennon-McCartney tunes and the brief pandemonium of adoration surrounding them. He connects us with the better parts of ourselves and the magic realm of imagination, defying the cares of the world with the mysterious power of song.

On this night, he opened his show with a stunning theatrical parade, as circus performers and costumed characters filtered through the audience. It was a way of clearing our minds and opening our eyes to the artistic landscape that lies behind the usual clutter. By the time he hit the opening chord to "Hello, Goodbye," Paul had us in his world.

It's a world filled with people like us. Who else on earth writes a pop song about a woman picking up rice in church after a wedding, with the lamenting refrain, "Ah, look at all the lonely people"?

Who else writes about a blackbird singing in the dead of night, waiting for its moment to be free?

And who else has had a Top 40 hit about a man facing his hour of darkness and seeing (his) mother Mary come to him, "speaking words of wisdom, let it be"?

Paul never has been overtly religious, but there is a great faith in life's goodness implicit in his songs. He seems to locate his faith in the artistic impulse. In a recent interview, he explained, "With creativity, I just have faith. ... It's a great spiritual belief that there's something really magical there."

He also is the most buoyant Beatle, bouncing back with almost annoying optimism from the rare hardships that come his way. On this U.S. tour, however, he exudes a new magnetism. He has lost Linda, his longtime love, as well as fellow Beatles George and John. We have lost a good deal of our innocence.

To see Paul back on stage, joyfully wailing "Can't Buy Me Love," reconnects us to hope and happiness we feared we had lost.

And so there was wonderful delight and affirmation in seeing insurance salesmen and grandparents boogie to "Lady Madonna," and hearing millennial 20-somethings sing along to "Hey Jude."

Thank you, Paul, for giving us joy in a hard world, and helping us believe we can work it out.

May 4, 2002

Playing for the Lord at the Y

The lobby of the David D. Hunting YMCA is bustling with rambunctious kids and afternoon athletes. But at a piano in the back, Chris Hubbard praises God in his own sweet-sounding world.

"How excellent is thy name, O Lord, how excellent is thy name," he sings, while pounding out majestic chords and dramatic flourishes on the keys of the Baldwin baby grand.

He ends with a powerful chord and a broad grin. "I love the joy of the Lord in music," he says.

Music is Chris Hubbard's joy — music and Jesus. He shares both with patrons of the downtown Y, who often hear him playing tunes with remarkable flair and facility.

Like "I'll Be Home for Christmas," with its rich, romantic chords, and "Frosty the Snowman," which he plunks out playfully while a woman bounces her clapping grandchild on her knee. And if you've not heard his riveting rendition of "O Holy Night" — well, that's worth a Y membership right there.

Hubbard is practicing holiday songs for a Christmas Eve breakfast for the homeless at First United Methodist Church. But his passion for piano is year-round and soul-deep.

He pursues it before and after workouts at the Y, where he strengthens his body and revives his spirit — a spirit he almost lost to years of alcoholism and homelessness.

Hubbard's spirit soars at the piano, his long-lost friend.

"All the years that I was an alcoholic and a smoker, I was not playing the piano very much at all," says Hubbard, 51, a church pianist in his younger days. "But when I gave my life back to Jesus, I started playing the piano again, and a lot of joy came back that was missing."

The joy of his playing reverberates through the Y, where he is the most frequent guest at the piano donated by the David D.

Hunting Jr. family. YMCA piano students sometimes use it for performances. Mostly, patrons play for fun or practice.

The first time Hubbard sat down to play, he "just enthralled all of us," recalls Stephanie Maloley, a YMCA membership services staffer.

"You can tell what mood he's in when he's playing," Maloley says. "Sometimes it's really dramatic.

"You can see he's working things out. Sometimes it's light as a feather, and it's just hauntingly beautiful."

The beauty has graced the sanctuary at First UMC, the downtown church where music director Mark Loring first heard Hubbard practicing. Hubbard has done day jobs there in a church-sponsored work program.

"I was like, 'Who is this guy? He's got some great chops,'" Loring recalls. "He's a talented guy, a real gospel pianist."

Loring gave Hubbard some sheet music and invited him to play preludes for a worship service. Hubbard also played at a November event celebrating the work program.

The church gigs provide much-needed cash. Hubbard gets by on disability payments for a leg injury, the result of a gunshot wound in what he calls "the iron jungle" of his drinking and drifting days. He prefers not to discuss those days, adding, "I want to leave it behind me."

While he still has his struggles, his companion on the continuing journey is the piano, which he affectionately calls "my best friend."

He sometimes plays in the lobby at Ferguson Apartments, a residence for homeless people with physical and mental disabilities where he lives. It's healing music for Hubbard when he gets frustrated with life, says Susan Gill, senior resident services coordinator.

"The piano is definitely a therapeutic thing for him," Gill says. "It just soothes his soul. It soothes my soul."

It has soothed mine as well when I have gone to the Y. After a hard morning at work, it is a gift to hear Hubbard's flamboyant playing filling the lobby with energy and grace.

When I asked him about the gift's source, he told me about an inspiring piano teacher he had growing up in Houston. Among the songs she taught him is a dazzler called "O Policinelo," which was the legendary Arthur Rubenstein's favorite encore.

To hear Hubbard hammer out its skittering, incredibly rapid notes is to wonder how a man this talented ever got away from the piano. But after years of playing for charismatic churches and in a Christian band, he says, "My life just kind of went to pieces for a while."

Losing his mother to a car crash and his wife to divorce, Hubbard wandered the country until a California pastor invited him into a church rehab program seven years ago.

He kicked alcohol, accepted Christ and started "living for God once again."

"It is miraculous that I actually came back to God and Jesus," he says. "If I hadn't, I'd probably be dead by now.

"I'm alive and breathing," he adds, and laughs. "But, spiritually, I'm alive and breathing, too."

It's good to see a man laugh with the joy of life renewed, and good to hear his spirit breathe through music. Especially at Christmas, we all could use a little more hope and cheer.

Chris Hubbard offers just that, because he got it from Jesus.

O holy night, indeed.

Dec. 23, 2007

Songs of faith comfort the grieving

Family and friends of John Kadela mingled in the lobby of the Catholic Parish of the Holy Spirit, exchanging smiles and quiet stories before his funeral.

Two picture boards told a story in snapshots of his 87 years: as a toddler holding hands with his folks; brandishing his first baseball bat; in uniform during World War II; dancing with his wife, Helen.

Mr. Kadela's body lay peacefully among yellow roses, a crucifix and an American flag, smartly dressed in a bow tie, holding a rosary and a cherry Dum Dums sucker. As an usher, he always gave out candy to kids after 8 a.m. Mass.

Such was the man whose life on Earth and in heaven they came to celebrate with memories, Scripture and song. As the Mass of Christian Burial began, it was the music that seemed to bring forth the tears of grandchildren, and perhaps give Helen a little extra strength, as they walked to the front pew.

"Surely the presence of the Lord is in this place, I can feel his mighty power and his grace," sang cantor David McWatters, his soothing, rich voice filling the light-filled sanctuary.

Emotions flowed freely as the pallbearers brought in Mr. Kadela's now-closed casket while McWatters led worshipers in a moving hymn taken from Isaiah: "And he will raise you up on eagles' wings, bear you on the breath of dawn, make you to shine like the sun and hold you in the palm of his hand."

The grandchildren picked that song as a fitting tribute to Mr. Kadela's bright spirit, said granddaughter Amanda Coleman in an eloquent reflection. "Grandpa certainly shone like the sun," she said, fighting back tears.

As cantor for this funeral, McWatters had a clear view of the family struggling with their emotions. He could empathize all too well.

"I see in their faces not just their faces, but the faces of everyone who's lost someone dear to them," McWatters said later. "I know someday it's going to be my family sitting in that front pew. So I'm singing for all of them — all of the faithfully departed."

McWatters sings for many funerals at Holy Spirit, his West Side Grand Rapids parish, as well as at other churches. He leads the songs that powerfully express the sorrow of death yet uplift with faith in the life to come.

"What I hope is that the music and the words will help people in their grief, but also help them in their faith," said McWatters, who has sung at funerals for 25 years. "These songs are the story of our faith."

It's a story that will be told about all of us someday. Cantors like McWatters play a key role in singing the story that takes us home after all our other stories have been told.

I've often been struck by how much I learn about people at their funerals. The reflections of ministers, family and friends bring forth the particular, often surprising, details that distinguished their lives.

The songs, meanwhile, bring forth the strong emotional mix of sadness over losing a loved one, appreciation for the joy he or she brought us, and honor for their sacred passage across the final river.

"Even though you have a sense of sadness and sorrow, these songs still lift you up because this isn't the end," said the Rev. John Vallier, Holy Spirit's pastor. "I've been at many funerals, from infants to adults, and it's amazing how people can sing even though their hearts are heavy."

For McWatters, singing for the heavy-hearted is a form of prayer. Director of Holy Spirit's Rite of Christian Initiation of Adults program for new church members, he leads the singing at many funerals along with a special "Resurrection Choir."

He takes the role seriously, spending time in prayer and researching the lives of the deceased beforehand. Sometimes he finds it tough to get through the songs, as when he sang "Battle Hymn of the Republic" for a young firefighter who died of cancer.

The funerals of children and teens are the hardest, says McWatters, who is a water polo and swimming coach at Rockford High School. Life is short, he tells his athletes. Make it count.

John Kadela's life was long, but its end was still painful for his loved ones. As they followed his casket out of the sanctuary, McWatters and the choir sang him home: "Come! Live in the light! Shine with the joy and the love of the Lord!"

It was a moving moment, heart-breaking in its finality, inspiring in its love.

May 28, 2011

Carols bring joy to a bruised world

As I walked through downtown Grand Rapids one lunch hour, something important was missing.

Greenery hung on the old buildings: check. Smiling passers-by: very nice. Enticing merchandise in the store windows: as always.

But! No music. No scratchy speakers blaring tinny versions of "Hark, the Herald Angels Sing." No strolling carolers. No sidewalk buskers tooting their trumpets. It was, like, way too quiet.

Dear city fathers, please fix this fast, if you have not done so already. This Christmas, more than ever, I want to be serenaded as I stroll. I want to hum "The First Noel" as I chomp my bagel. My soul craves the carols of old.

Happily, I have done plenty of singing this holiday season. And wherever I have done my singing, I notice others singing with joy as grateful as mine. We all seem to hunger for music as if it were a steaming bowl of bread pudding.

Of course we do. We are very tired this holiday season. We have been beat up pretty badly this year. Pilgrims assaulted in the dark, we seek solace and healing in song.

We're all weary travelers stopping by the country inn. We sidle up to the bar, glance over at the piano player and say, "Hey, do you know 'White Christmas?'"

Thank goodness for those gifted musicians who do know "White Christmas" and a zillion other holiday tunes both sacred and saccharine. They reconnect us to the lovely past and to the warm places inside that make us sing with big silly grins.

At St. Andrew's Cathedral one Friday evening, music lovers streamed into the hallowed place until they filled its 800 or so seats. The rest spent 90 minutes on their feet to hear the Western Michigan University choir and orchestra perform Poulenc,

Rutter and a really nifty version of "Sleigh Ride." They all stood for the Hallelujah Chorus of Handel's "Messiah," apparently our spiritual national anthem.

At the Grand Rapids Symphony's Holiday Pops concert, harpist Elizabeth Wooster mesmerized the place by pulling strands of heaven down from above and gently draping them over all of us. The orchestra's snappy "Winter Wonderland" was an animated Currier and Ives print. We crooned with gusto on the sing-alongs, even on that corny reindeer tune.

My most memorable singing along, though, was with Garrison Keillor. As I drove through the dark one Saturday night, he led his "Prairie Home Companion" audience in a rendition of "Silver Bells." I actually sang in my car, doubtless along with thousands of other solitary listeners who sought a bit of old-fashioned cheer.

The sentimental strains fell softly on my spirit like snowflakes, as such songs usually do. Music speaks a wholly other language to us, made of memories, longings and resonant intimations of a great goodness connecting us all. It is a wonderful human expression that the mere strum of a guitar can diminish differences and create community.

I am not fussy about the faith issues of song this time of year. At my son's public-school holiday concert, I can't imagine many were not glad to sing along on "Joy to the World." To water down public holiday singing with praises to St. Nick up on the rooftop is rather insulting to the whole spirit of the thing.

Santa songs are fine, for fun. But I need to sing "Angels We Have Heard on High" to stir the strings of my heart. I'd much rather join in on a rousing Hanukkah tune than be banished to a safely secular public square with nary a manger in sight.

The events of these past months call me to sing "O Come, All Ye Faithful" more joyfully than ever, as others sing of their faiths. In singing, our hearts beat a little stronger and our courage grows a little braver. The ancient bells ring again, calling us to bow down and bless all this eternal goodness, however bruised we feel.

Be quiet and be blessed, the angels sing. Stop running around. Don't sweat the details. You are still here, and so are we. Life is still good. In excelsis Deo.

When I was a child, we sang carols around the piano on Christmas Eve. I miss those childhood songs this Christmas. I want to sing them again, and see Bethlehem lying still, its people in a deep and dreamless sleep as the silent stars go by.

Surely on that night a little boy stood on some street corner, looked up and said, "Yes, I see you, God. Mind if I sing?"

Dec. 22, 2001

On top of the world, dreaming

As I run downhill into the great wide green park, a Tom Petty song pours through my ear buds:

I got someone who loves me tonight
I got over $1,000 in a bank, and I'm all right
Look deep in the eyes of love
And find out what you were looking for
I got a room at the top of the world tonight
And I ain't comin' down

My running takes me past a couple chatting by a pond, parents pushing little ones in strollers, a woman laying out picnic fixings. I'm pulled by the sights before me and the sounds playing in my head.

The body obeys my will, legs pumping, lungs huffing, skin sweating. It's a minor miracle I am still running after all these years. My knees should be gone by now, or my wind, or my will. But someone ran before me, showing me the way.

Running under the mighty maple and oak trees of the park, I feel sheltered by their roof of leaves and their ancient strength. I always run underneath them in an invisible path known only to me.

My iPod summons "He's Gone Away," a lovely instrumental by Pat Metheny and Charlie Haden, just as I am passing by a picnic table in a tree-sheltered glade. I know I must stop and sit here.

This is the tune we played at my father's memorial service as soundtrack to a slideshow of his life. My sister chose it because it was this album, "Beyond the Missouri Sky," that gave her comfort night after night following Mom and Dad's passing.

I first sit, then lie on the rough wooden table, looking up through the canopy of leaves at the sky above. Patches of bright blue are flecked with soft white clouds blowing by from north to south. Here, the sky speaks to my mind.

I love this sky because Dad taught me to; I adore these mighty trees because he fought forest fires as a young man; rest from my running because he circled the track every day between classes at MSU.

I love listening to this song because Mom played "Won't You Come Home, Bill Bailey?" and "Moonlight on Vermont" on the baby grand piano she inherited from grandma, who played ragtime at the New Year's Eve parties.

The sun starts to glow behind a cloud, then breaks clear into open sky, gloriously, blinking through the roof of leaves overhead. I weep because this is the heart they gave me, easily moved by the mystery of the world and the emotions welling deep inside.

All these feelings, gifts, inclinations, wonderings, came from them to me. And all of it came from God, through Mom and Dad, through me, to my children, to all my loved ones.

Why do I say it all comes from God? Because I choose to. It is one of the few decisions over which I have any say, and I say it every day.

My iPod summons U2, and I know I must lie a moment longer:

I was speeding on the subway
Through the stations of the cross
Every eye looking every other way
Counting down till the pain will stop
At the moment of surrender
Of vision over visibility
I did not notice the passersby
And they did not notice me

The breeze dries my tears and cools my sweat. I sit up. No one is passing by. It is time to run again.

So run I do. It's what I was made for.

Soulmailing, June 22, 2012

Al Green finds love and happiness

Near the end of his sold-out show at Frederik Meijer Gardens & Sculpture Park Monday night, Al Green wiped the sweat from his eyes and paused from singing his 1971 hit, "Tired of Being Alone."

"There's some people here saying, 'I wonder if Al Green's still got it?'" said the legendary soul singer, who at age 66 has been turning out hits longer than many in his audience have been alive.

Green then let out a long, impassioned wail in his trademark falsetto that left no doubt he has still has it. The crowd of 1,900 fans erupted in cheers. Green shed his dark jacket and tossed out more of the red roses with which he festooned the crowd all night long.

Those who knew Green during his formative years in Grand Rapids could have told you long ago that the ambitious young man from Arkansas definitely had what it takes to be a pop star. What wasn't as clear was whether his upbringing in the church would stick through the wild distractions of fame.

He's seen plenty of the latter, including a girlfriend's much-publicized assault and suicide in 1974. But the fact that the Rev. Green today preaches from the pulpit of his Memphis church, while still wailing the R&B hits that get people dancing, gratifies those who knew him when.

"He did what he had to do, but the Lord kept him, even so," said the Rev. Charlie Jones, pastor of Macedonia Missionary Baptist Church, who was Green's youth choir director back in the day at Gospel Temple Baptist Church. "That's very hard for some people. I don't know anybody else could have kept him."

Then Jones added with an admiring chuckle, "I'll tell you what, he's got it."

Lee Virgins, a onetime member of Green's first pop group, also saw that star wattage in his boyhood pal. Virgins sang at clubs around the Midwest with Al Greene and the Creations, a group Green formed in high school before dropping the last "e" from his name.

"I could see the potential that Al had," said Virgins, 70, of Grand Rapids. "I knew that if he lived and didn't lose his voice, he was going to be something big."

But Virgins, who sang on Green's first hit, "Back Up Train," also saw an element of faith in the golden-voiced young man he regarded as a younger brother, and for whom he acted as a kind of chaperone on the tough streets of 1960s Grand Rapids.

"The church was always in Al's heart," said Virgins, who heard Green's first sermon at Full Gospel Tabernacle, where Green was ordained pastor in 1976. "I don't know if he can preach as well as he can sing, but he knows the Word."

The Word of God was a key part of Green's upbringing. Beginning at age 9, he sang in a family gospel quartet, the Greene Brothers, in his hometown of Forrest City, Ark. The group continued to perform with Green's father, Robert, after the family moved to Grand Rapids in the mid-1950s.

It was in this gritty northern city that young Al lost his innocence but found his passion for singing. There began the battle for what Green describes in his autobiography as "the no-man's-land in my soul, separating the sacred and profane."

In "Take Me to the River," Green recalls his first impressions of Grand Rapids as a dirty, smelly city. It brought tears to his eyes with the memory of Arkansas' pine forests and hardened his heart with a "mean and vindictive streak." Beaten up by a bully at Franklin Elementary School, the next day he conked the kid with a Coke bottle to establish his don't-mess-with-me identity.

But it was also at Franklin where he found his voice, singing to himself before class one day only to find a crowd listening to him in the doorway. With help from a kind choir director, he found his joy.

"The music transported me, and the sound of my own singing was another kind of power," he writes. "Up on that stage, raising my voice to the rafters ... was a way of marking my place in the world, of standing firm and proclaiming loud and clear, 'My name is Al Greene, and I am somebody!'"

Besides singing at Gospel Temple, he sang at revivals with Mother Bates, matriarch of the storefront House of Prayer, who taught him about caring for the poor and loving one's enemy.

But this was the '60s, and the lure of rock and roll and soul singers like Jackie Wilson made church seem boring by comparison.

The glamor of "bright lights and beautiful women" temporarily took over the no-man's land, and his father kicked Al out of his gospel group.

Rev. Jones says Green told him at one point, "'Deacon Jones, I'm going out and make a million, and then I'm coming back to Christianity.' I said I'd be praying for him till he gets back."

More than 20 million gospel and pop records later, the Rev. Green has long been back in church but still sings with soul — God and the devil dueling it out in one incredible voice. At Meijer Gardens, many in the crowd held up their open hands as he sang a white-hot "Amazing Grace," then boogied and sang along with his No. 1 hit, "Let's Stay Together."

With his blazing smile and spine-shivering voice, it was impossible to see where the preacher left off and the soul singer took over. To me, my boogie partner, Andrea, and the other 1,900, it didn't much matter.

What he sang was joy, and what we hummed into the night was "Love and Happiness."

June 19, 2012

Dylan: prophetic poet, elusive jester

The other day I sat down and listened to a folk song written 36 years ago, and its prophetic power whacked me between the eyes.

How many times must a man look up before he can see the sky? Yes and how many ears must one man have before he can hear people cry? Yes and how many deaths will it take till he knows that too many people have died? The answer, my friend, is blowing in the wind.

With his paltry guitar and homely, nasal voice, Bob Dylan sang these words that have not lost a whit of relevance since the traumatic time when he first sang them. "Blowin' in the Wind" appeared on Dylan's second album in 1963, the year in which the JFK assassination ended a generation's innocence.

A year later, Dylan issued a more ominous notice of the upheaval that was soon to come:

Come mothers and fathers throughout the land, and don't criticize what you can't understand. Your sons and your daughters are beyond your command ... For the times, they are a-changin'.

For the wide-eyed '60s child back then, that was a stirring battle cry of some vague revolution that soon would change everything for the better. To the middle-aged dad now, it is easy to imagine the chill it sent through our parents' bones.

Dylan did not sing either of those songs at his Van Andel Arena concert Monday night. But he did sing "Gotta Serve Somebody" with its blunt challenge, "Might be the devil, might be the Lord, but we all got to serve somebody." And he sang "Masters of War," that scathing indictment of militarism, while some in the audience fetched themselves a drink. Mostly, he sang rock 'n' roll, while grandparents and 20-somethings shook and danced hippie-style.

As always, Dylan was almost totally uncommunicative, except through his songs. And aside from witnessing an enjoyable concert, it was difficult to discern which way the wind was blowing.

Dylan the prophet, Dylan the jester, Dylan the hermit, Dylan the country boy, Dylan the born-again Christian: The man has changed his persona as frequently as the times themselves have changed since that first burst of clear-eyed mid-'60s idealism. He clearly does not want to give us easy answers; he leaves us to figure them out for ourselves.

Oh, for a '90s prophet who could point us toward change as convincingly as Dylan once did. But if we did have one, would we have ears enough to hear him?

The most prophetic popular music of this decade may be rap music, both reflecting the ugly realities of the street and pointing toward the changing face of youth culture. It's not a form of prophecy to which I care to listen. But then, there were times I didn't care to listen to Dylan either.

Like many others, I dismissed the Jewish-born Dylan as having "gone Christian" when he embraced Christ on his 1979 album, "Slow Train Coming." Songs like "Gotta Serve Somebody" did not serve the sensibilities of those who, like me, had thrown the church out with the bath water during the '60s. Established religion was at least as suspect as established capitalism to people seeking Utopia.

Yet there was always a religious element to Dylan's work, lyrically and musically. In the Christian journal Books & Culture, Wheaton College professor Alan Jacobs writes, "In Dylan, the prophet meets the bluesman: the ancient laments of Israel rejoin songs born in slavery." He calls Dylan "a key figure in the social history of American religion," and argues that in his Christian conversion, "the prophetic voice had discovered a genuine source."

Dylan downplayed his beliefs after a few albums, spent some time with an Orthodox Jewish group and retreated back into his enigmatic shell. But he revealed much in a 1991 interview when asked if he were happy. "It's not happiness or unhappiness, it's either blessed or unblessed," Dylan said. "As the Bible says, 'Blessed is the man who walketh not in the counsel of the ungodly.'"

Now that I have children and have taken the spiritual lumps of changing times, I find myself more open to the whole range of Dylan's work, whether sacred or profane, "Desolation Row" or "Dignity." Perhaps he is no longer a prophet; maybe he never really was. As always, he leaves me searching for my own answers, and hoping they don't blow away in the wind.

Feb. 20, 1999

Medema colors the world with song

As a boy on Grand Rapids' West Side, Ken Medema would stick a speaker in his attic window and play Christmas music for the neighborhood.

The Robert Shaw Chorale, Mantovani's Christmas album or some other favorite would drift down 11th Street NW on deep snowy days. He wanted the whole neighborhood to share in the joy he felt in that music.

"I loved the music," Medema recalls warmly. "I loved to go to every Christmas program there was."

It was mostly through music that Medema experienced the magic of Christmas. Music, midnight Mass, and the scents of conifers and candles.

When his parents took him to sit on Santa's lap at Herpolsheimer's department store, he could just make out the white of Santa's beard. He could see white lights on a Christmas tree but not the colored ones. Born blind, Medema has always seen the world as black-and-white shadows.

But Christmas was, and is, a wonderful time for him, a season to be praised as Medema praises all life — with music.

"Let's go up into a holy place, let's go up into a dreaming space, vision coming like a summer rain, till the garden comes alive again."

Medema's elegant voice drifts from big speakers through a Jenison recording studio, where he's mixing his new CD. He stands between the speakers, leaning right and left, checking the balance of sounds. He taps his foot and pats his hand on his knee as a lush, sitar-backed praise song, "Sanctus," picks up steam.

He smiles as engineer Robert Reister brings up the sound of an oboe Medema created with his keyboard. "Oh, yeah!" Medema exclaims. "Whoo!"

"Are you happy?" asks Beverly Vander Molen, Medema's manager, when the song ends. "I think so," he replies.

I think so too. In my years of reporting on a motley mix of humankind, Ken Medema strikes me as one of the happier people I have met. Yet an awareness of pain comes through strongly in his gentle music, soft smile and booming laugh.

His tangible love of life and music have taken him from the world of music therapy, where he worked with disturbed children and teens, to a 27-year career as a Christian concert and recording artist. The most recent of his dozen albums is "All the Way to Bethlehem," a Christmas disc recorded last year.

For him, music has always been a way to bind people together, from his upbringing in Grand Rapids, through classes at Michigan State University to his home in San Francisco.

Over lunch hour at Grand Rapids Christian High School, Medema would play rock and roll tunes he had written. Dozens of students would gather to listen, while choir teacher Trena Haan, no fan of rock music, conveniently went somewhere else.

"It was the one thing that made me feel like I belonged," Medema tells me over breakfast at a busy Grandville diner. "There was so much I couldn't do. One of the ways of breaking through that barrier was singing rock and roll tunes."

He likes to think he also broke down barriers among the kids who came to listen, helping them find each other. He still tries to do that.

"Every time I get on stage, I have that feeling of being in the choir room," says Medema, 56 and the father of two. "I still have that sense of needing to find a way to make you like me, and needing to be the vehicle that brings people together."

But he also has been a restless Christian all along. He broke out of a don't-ask-questions Christian Reformed childhood, prodded by an inspirational piano teacher, Heather Halsted. She encouraged him to learn everything about everything, gave him a book on mythology and read him sermons by the fiercely independent Rev. Duncan Littlefair of Fountain Street Church. One day he met Littlefair, who told him, "Son, don't ever stop asking questions."

Medema eventually ended up in the progressive wing of the Baptist Church through his wife, Jane. Today, he says he is "much more Jesus-driven than what Heather would have liked." But he's also an inquiring musician who listens to rock artists like Nine Inch Nails and Fiona Apple along with jazz, classical and the latest in Christian contemporary.

Over breakfast, he questions how we celebrate Christmas.

"My primary experience of Christmas is that there's a lot of noise," he says. "There's almost an input overload for me."

Suddenly I'm aware of how much noise is in the diner, and how the world must sound to Medema. Wherever he goes, he hears not just noise, but the same songs he used to love as a child: Bing Crosby, "Jingle Bells."

"I long for silence," he says, and is surprised by the tears that well in his eyes.

"I'd love to see us have a quiet Advent. Advent is the quiet time when you proclaim hope, even when hope seems dead."

In the rush to celebrate Christmas, he says, we've skipped the hushed uncertainty leading up to it, the wonder that impregnates everyone with something wonderful and new.

"There always ought to be new questions at Advent ... new songs that take us into that domain where we know life is going to change, but we don't know how.

"That's really Advent. It's the not knowing. It's Mary and Jesus going to Bethlehem and saying, 'What in the world have we gotten ourselves into?'"

Only after they arrive is it time for Christmas, time to make music and celebrate what he calls "the radically new."

He makes the journey by taking long walks, thinking about the past year and what might be in store for him next year. He'll spend a quiet Christmas Eve with his family. Then comes Christmas morning, present-opening and the blessed week leading to New Year's.

"I just love that time," he says. "I can let go the silence, and run into the New Year and direction in my life with abandon."

He has a few things to take care of before then, though. Like adding the sound of rain at the end of "Sanctus." He listens to the track over and over, bobbing his head in time.

"So, you think it works?" he asks when it's over.

Yes, Ken, I think it works. It would sound great coming from an attic speaker.

Dec. 18, 1999

Fifth Inning

For the Beauty
of the Earth

Dewy mornings evoke faith of a child

Nothing evokes the sense of childhood revisited like a spring morning.

It's something about the birds singing so confidently, the dew on the grass, the sun not quite up yet. It all feels expectant, like something good will happen today, and the dew has washed away the fears of the night.

The bird songs remind me of my first morning in London in the summer of 1976. I woke up to the sound of schoolchildren walking below my window. Their delectable British accents made me smile with the recognition of something long forgotten: the joy of being alive.

This morning feels fresh like that. If I were to venture outside in my robe, the dew would soak my slippers. I would see flowers waiting patiently for the sun, and I could smell their naked fragrance.

As it is, I hear the long, melancholy horn of the train crossing through downtown, a childhood sound. A few minutes ago the bells of Sacred Heart Catholic Church pealed the general joy of Jesus, floating up from John Ball Park to my house on the hill.

I imagine the Catholic school kids walking by the park on their way to class in white shirts and plaid skirts. I remember as if it were yesterday my daughter, Emily, lining up for her first day of kindergarten there. She is now 26 and beginning to write her dissertation.

I remember waking up on mornings like this and walking to my safety post. Despite the official sash I wore, a bully punched me in the shoulder one day, leaving a knot of pain. Still, I manned my corner with the authority of an 8-year-old traffic cop.

I had probably slept well the night before. Children usually do. I went to sleep with an optimistic prayer:

"Now I lay me down to sleep, I pray the Lord my soul to keep.
Keep me safely through the night, Wake me by the morning light."

That was how we prayed in my house. None of this "If I should die before I wake, I pray the Lord my soul to take" jazz. That was too traditional and too scary for us. We were kinda sorta Unitarians, or as close to Unitarian as Fountain Street Church took you.

It was there I learned simple lessons of faith in Character School: treat all people with dignity, respect all faiths, and do right in all things. Not much, perhaps, by orthodox Christian standards, but it pointed me in the right direction faith-wise. So did the songs I learned there, like, "'Tis a gift to be simple, 'tis a gift to be free ..."

We did not memorize Bible verses. But then, formal religion is not that well suited to children anyway. They just want to know the basics: that God loves them, that they are safe, and life is going to be good.

That's how I usually felt waking up as a kid. I went to sleep dreaming of home runs and woke up feeling I could hit one.

I may have worshipped Al Kaline a little too much. But it was not a bad faith. It was the faith of new mornings in spring.

On a day like this, I would have been out the door early on my way to school. I walked a few blocks to Ottawa Hills Elementary, past the flowering trees, ready to learn whatever the teachers had for us that day.

I didn't know what I needed to know but had faith they would tell me.

Then, on Saturdays, I'd head out with bat and glove, with faith there was a game out there for me somewhere.

Oh, for that kind of faith this morning, with the dew still on the grass. I am not a kid anymore, God knows. But it is a new morning in spring, and life beckons like an empty ball diamond.

May 12, 2007

Gardening angels on their knees

The angels come walking up to Parish of the Holy Spirit, bearing flats of flowers and casserole dishes.

Here's Nan Smigiel carrying a tray of pink impatiens. M.J. Best totes a pasta salad. Up strides Abe Rossi wearing a T-shirt that reads, "Holy Spirit Garden Angels Men's Division."

Maggie Wind greets them all in a periwinkle sweatshirt ("Gardener Outstanding in My Field"), with watering-can earrings and a brooch of three golden angels. It's a cool, breezy morning at the Catholic church, and Holy Spirit's Garden Angels are ready to kneel and plant.

"They'll get wet knees, but that's OK," says Wind, 82, the smiling archangel of these devoted diggers.

She got them started about 10 years ago after planting a few flowers around the Pieta statue out front, depicting Mary holding the body of Christ. The next year, church ushers gave her $300 to plant more.

She recruited fellow gardeners, and soon the Garden Angels, as they call themselves, came into being.

"We all love to garden, and we love each other," says Ruth Levanduski, who particularly loves irises.

They meet each Wednesday at the church to plant and maintain the gardens on Holy Spirit's ample grounds. Afterward, they gather for a prayer and lunch. They call it "angel food."

"Another thing about these gals, they're all good cooks," says Rossi, already looking forward to the meal at 9 a.m.

There's a dozen angels this morning, with Rossi and Jim Larsen the only guys. "This is my harem, but they work me to death," Abe cracks.

No one minds the work. Quite the opposite.

M.J. Best is on her knees planting butterfly daisies, which poke up their cheery yellow petals around an American flag.

"They're the only ones I don't mind dead-heading," Best says as she snips off wilted blooms. "Oh, when they blossom they just look so perky and fresh."

Digging a wet hole with her spade, she reflects on the pleasure of hearing people comment as they leave Mass.

"You feel like you're doing something for the church, and for God," she says. "It makes the church beautiful for the people who are coming here."

Such beauty there is in a flower, says Wind, who has been growing them most of her life. She tends a garden at her home just across Lake Michigan Drive NW. She even grew a World War II victory garden when she was a teen.

We walk by the Pieta, surrounded by a palette of bright yellow pansies, pink impatiens, purple and white petunias.

"Did you ever look at a flower, how God made that flower?" Wind says, opening her hands as if holding one. "All the parts to it and how beautiful it is?

"I always say, 'God made weeds to keep us on our knees.'"

She prayed plenty last year while battling cancer. She was too weak to plant her garden then, so the Garden Angels planted it for her. It was only fitting; Wind often takes flowers to parishioners in nursing homes.

Past the hostas Wind planted along the front walk, Nan Smigiel and Sue Swartz are on their knees planting impatiens next to the school. Their pantlegs are soaked, and their gloves dirt-caked.

Smigiel loves being away from phones, listening to the birds and wind chimes.

"It's pretty peaceful out here," she says.

"We've got some extra impatiens," she tells Wind. "You want them down there by the cross?"

"On the edge, yes," says Wind.

Wind and other angels plan the garden design each spring, then, flush with the parish flower fund, look for deals in area nurseries.

"We see flowers, we stop," Wind says. "We make U-turns, too."

We're in the courtyard garden, adorned with colorful birdhouses made by students. A statue of a smiling Mary, holding a smiling Jesus, serenely gazes on the pink peonies and star-shaped clematis.

Dodie Poniatowski, an active angel who is away helping her daughter this day, normally tends the courtyard as well as the rose garden tucked behind the rectory. Deep red blooms surround a statue of St. Fiacre, patron saint of gardens. The late Ruth Esler, a prominent rosarian, planted this in memory of her husband, John.

Wind surveys the abundant beauty surrounding Holy Spirit and marvels at what God can do in a single flower.

"When did he find time to design this?" she asks with a chuckle, then answers herself. "It's God. He can do anything."

June 12, 2010

There's no time but the present

Time finally came to a stop for me, one perfect afternoon in Northport.

I was sitting on a bench in front of an antique store. Next to me, my son slugged down a can of pop. Across the street, an American flag stuck on a tree stirred slightly in the breeze.

A guy stopped his truck and walked into a bakery. A couple strolled by in no hurry at all. A group of boys briefly circled on their bicycles, then moved on.

They appeared like figures in a painting or a scene from a Sherwood Anderson novel. For a moment, stillness descended. A reverie of nothing changing, like the past and present were one, as if I were watching a memory as it happened.

I snapped out of it shortly, probably about the time my wife and daughter came by and we all headed into an ice cream parlor. But the timeless feeling clung to me as the tattered screen doors swung to. Unvarnished wooden floors, wire-backed chairs, a peanut butter grinder all seemed from another time. Perfect Resort Town 1955.

Did time take a detour around Northport? Or had we just stepped into the Twilight Zone?

Forgive my romanticizing of a place whose charms most readers probably have known for years. I'd never had the pleasure, despite most of a lifetime in Michigan. We were only there a couple of hours, but it felt like a long time. Here was a place where I could sit reading in a used bookstore while the women proprietors chatted as if I were a boarder.

Somebody take me back, please.

The truth is, that little Northport moment just distilled a week of hovering around the bliss of Grand Traverse Bay. Which was just a distillation of something I'd been looking for all summer: a way to slow down time.

Time has only been speeding up for the past decade of my life. Months get chewed up like Bazooka gum, weeks fly away like scared partridges, days are nothing but blinks. Had a lousy Fourth of July? Just hang on a second, it'll be back soon.

This trend reached ridiculous proportions this spring, probably having something to do with my 45th birthday. So after school let out, I simply quit doing stuff. Every day without something written on the calendar was a little victory. Evenings were reserved for important things, like riding bikes or going down to Sullivan Field to watch a ball game.

But of course life still had structure. I still had to be someplace around 8:30 a.m. or I'd wind up a paper boy instead of a reporter. It took a week at Grand Traverse, without a wristwatch, to leave time behind.

This has to do with more than just breaking from the tyranny of routine, I believe. A week at Jellystone Campground has few reminders of time, except the soothing PA voice at 11 p.m. saying goodnight.

Instead, what camping and the bay remind me of is how illusory time is. There's a time to wake and a time to sleep, a time to eat and a time for Yogi and Boo-Boo to clean up the campground. But none of it has much to do with clocks. Twelve o'clock noon is only a time because we decide it is; it doesn't exist on Grand Traverse Bay.

A watch on the beach is an abomination against nature.

Time here is a process, not a schedule. It's the sweetness of the air in the morning, the lazy big sky at midday, and the rich colors over dark choppy water at sunset.

It's wading into the incredibly cold water when you're hot, diving into the waves when you're brave enough, seeing the sailboats bob for miles out when you emerge. Then back on the beach to get buried in cool damp sand, or read till you sweat then back in the water. And so on.

Out at Old Mission Point, time is precious while you spend it walking barefoot on the shore, watching a dad in the waves holding his toddler while his wife snaps their picture. Glancing up at the lighthouse, out at the mighty lake, down at gleaming stones. This is the gospel of nature, reminding us gently of earth's ancient beauty.

I picked up a smooth gray pebble and pocketed it. When we got back Saturday, I set it next to my alarm clock.

There it stays, under the red digital numbers, silently reminding me of a world beyond time.

July 26, 1997

Going deep in the season of change

The boys were scattered across the Union High gridiron, eight to a side, tossing a football in the rapidly dying light of an early autumn evening.

Receivers took off in seven directions, each with a boy defending him. The quarterback surveyed his options, chose an open man and fired the pigskin at him. Caught! Then the boy hit the turf with another lad wrapped around his legs.

Watching their pickup game from the hill up above, I could remember the smell of the cool, damp grass as he landed. I could recall the sounds of the boy-game — "Go deep!" "I'm open!" — and the magic of playing after the lights came on, until the ball was so indistinct it hit you in the chest by the time you saw it.

This is distinctly American autumn, this playing of football and bringing home grass stains. Our seasonal life is tied to planting and cultivating and harvesting. But it's also bound up in sports, which lend their own ritual rhythms to that of the earth.

Here, in early October, the rhythm of sports mingles for me with the change in the air.

Football is well under way with its pounding action and hysterical hoopla, blanket-covered fans cheering while clutching hot chocolate.

Baseball is reaching the heart-stopping drama of the playoffs, pitchers facing down sluggers with the bases loaded, bleary-eyed fans commiserating over coffee the next morning.

And all the while, days become shorter, leaves grow brighter and the moon looms larger. The mornings are chilly enough to throw a comforter on. Everything is restless, changing. Things are dying. And yet so much is starting up.

It fills me with warm memory but also unsettles me. Autumn means change, and change means uncertainty.

I prefer certainty. But I also relish the mystery of change and the whisper of wind-scattered leaves.

I have been reading about fall's deeper dimensions in "Autumn: A Spiritual Biography of the Season," published by Skylight Paths.

Its editors, Calvin College literature professors Gary Schmidt and Susan Felch, offer a sampling of seasonal essays as they did in their previous rumination on winter.

Schmidt and Felch call it "the season of inconstancy," full of "shifting landscapes and experiences."

They write of its bright maples, state fairs and pungent dry leaves, and the challenge of staying spiritually centered while fall "juggles blazing opposites in a great circle."

The book's three dozen authors range from the expected — Thoreau, Frost, Keats —to the delightfully diverse. The medieval mystic Julian of Norwich finds God's love in a hazelnut. Tracy Kidder sees spiritual strength in a fifth-grade teacher beginning the school year.

Kentucky writer Wendell Berry, exploring the terrain of his farm, finds himself "worshipful in its presence."

He senses his mortality in falling leaves and the promise of rebirth in the "Christ-like" topsoil: "It is enriched by all the things that die and enter into it."

A. Bartlett Giamatti, the late baseball commissioner and former president of Yale, offers a melancholy essay on the Boston Red Sox losing yet another pennant race. Baseball is "designed to break your heart," he writes, as only a Bosox fan can. It begins with the newness of spring, offers the promise of endless summer, then "leaves you to face the fall all alone."

"Dame Mutability never loses," Giamatti writes. And of course, the Red Sox always do.

For me, fall rounds out a season that began in Florida with my father. We watched the Tigers lob long, lazy tosses under a bright sun. Everything was new and summer seemed to stretch out forever. Anything was possible.

Now, reality reasserts itself. The Tigers will not be in the playoffs, although I will watch those games late into the night.

Soon the leaves will fall, and the crack of the bat will be just a memory for the long winter.

So I watch the boys play football, and remember how it felt to be 13 and going deep.

A light wind from the west touches my face. In it, I seem to smell burning leaves, hot apple pies and just a trace of winter ice.

Change is on the way. It makes me restless and a little anxious. But I also welcome it, because Dame Mutability can be quite beautiful.

Oct. 2, 2004

Postscript: On Oct. 27, 2004, the Boston Red Sox defeated the St. Louis Cardinals for their first World Series title in 86 years.

Up North, land of magical pines

Near our old family cabin on the Muskegon River was a grove of pines that led to a magic world.

I would walk the narrow trail between them and feel protected by their green, whispering canopy. Snowflakes drifted down with special gracefulness. Sunlight glinted through with unusual clarity.

It was a transporting place, like stepping into the wardrobe to Narnia.

The cool thing is, I have found this same place in other places since then. Take me to a grove of pines, and again, I'm transported to a world where the snow speaks and the trees whisper — Up North.

We all know where that is. It's not so much a location as a realm of the imagination. It's where trees sigh overhead, snow crunches underfoot, embers burn deep into the night and nothing where you come from really matters.

It's a Michigan thing, made of tar-paper cabins and gravel roads and great stands of woods. It is the pull of what Jack London called the forest primeval.

I feel its pull strongly now, in the still beauty of a long winter.

I felt it last weekend, on a rare walk with my dad through the nature trails surrounding Lake Lansing.

This is nowhere near Up North geographically. But here again, we came upon a grove of pines: Scots, red and Norway spruce. My, they were something: tall and slender and strong. We walked through them as through a cathedral.

They put my dad in mind of when he was a kid and his folks hauled him out of Detroit to a rustic cabin near Batchawana Bay in Ontario.

He recalled once sitting alone in Hartwick Pines State Park, breathing in the soft fragrance of virgin white pine. Suddenly, he felt the presence of his parents, long passed by that time, as if they were right there with him.

It put me in mind of my childhood sojourns Up North with Dad and my family. I, too, had spiritual revelations in the woods.

For me, Up North began at Open Hamburgers. This was what we called the Whitehouse Restaurant, where, about 8 p.m. on a Friday night, we would pile in cold and famished on our way to the cabin. No burger and fries have tasted as delicious since. Its neon sign burned like a beacon in the night: "Open Hamburgers."

Then, it was another hour into the forest primeval, our headlights boring a white tunnel into the blackness of tree-lined gravel roads. Dad kept his braking foot ready for the glint of deer's eyes.

Then to the cabin itself, tucked among white birches — you never felt such cold. Dead, penetrating cold, seeping into my bones as I hurriedly threw logs onto the fire grate. There I'd stand for an hour, the roaring flames baking my back while my breath steamed the air.

Winter weekends I seldom strayed far from the fire. I drank coffee and wolfed down Tolkien, Heinlein and Hugo. Their tales transported my mind far from our bluff above the Muskegon.

When I ventured outside, it was invariably to the grove of pines, and to a bend in the river where the trees stood especially tall. Here I'd stand and drink in the quiet majesty of creation.

Here, for the first time, I felt the spiritual stirring of something greater than myself. I sensed the wonder of the world and wondered where it came from. I knew I was part of it but wasn't sure which part. I just knew I felt at home with it.

I wouldn't have said so then, but God was getting to me. The voice of the creator was speaking through the rushing of the river and the whooshing of the trees.

Maybe the fisher hears the same in the sleepy lapping of waves, or the hiker in the lonely crack of a branch.

Surely that's part of what pulls us Up North — to hear that quiet voice, far from the noise of our lives; then warm ourselves by the fire.

March 5, 2005

Skiing getaway yields blessed contact

MANISTEE NATIONAL FOREST, AWAY FROM PEOPLE — We were skiing through the woods, my dad and I, with that lovely *shoosh* sound cross-country skis make on new snow. That and my breathing were all I heard until I came to a stop and listened to ... nothing.

Maybe the muffled roar of a far-off snowmobile or a dog's lonely bark. A few bird chirps. Stubborn wrinkled oak leaves stirring in the wind. Mostly, blessed quiet.

This is how Dad and I wanted it. Just us, out in the woods, with few other people around. We do this once a year, go up to a swell little cabin near the little burg of Wellston and cruise the groomed trails of the "Big M" ski area. It's a chance to commune with nature and reconnect with each other.

Oh, we like running into the odd person here and there. In the Big M warming hut, we ran into a guy who my father had as a student at Michigan State University 25 years ago, and who used to work with one of my best friends. People like him we were delighted to meet.

Otherwise, the fewer people the better. We didn't really need them for our getaway. Just us and the snow were good enough.

As I *shooshed* through the woods, I found myself slipping in and out of the glide zone — the mental terrain where I was focused on the moment, the soft pine boughs and woodpecker-ravaged stumps and good cold air.

Out of the glide zone, I thought about stories I was working on, kid problems, what I wanted for dinner. Ski while you're skiing, I reminded myself. Later, eat while you're eating.

It wasn't long before we got to that eating part and spun out of the glide zone like a Pinto on black ice.

We'd driven into Manistee for dinner when a woman pulled alongside our Ford Explorer. "You've got a flat tire!" she yelled, pointing at the wheel. We'll call her Good Samaritan No. 1.

We pulled into a parking lot and had a look. "Yep, she's flat all right," we said. We got out the spare and the jack and went to work. I grabbed the tire iron and started loosening lug nuts. One, two, three ... hmm, this baby's a toughie. Maybe if I put my shoulder into it and give 'er a real good yank ...

(I can hear all the grease monkeys yelling, "DON'T DO IT!!")

Yank! Oops. That lug nut looked like a piece of crushed tin foil. Time to call AAA.

Good Samaritan No. 2, a clerk at a nearby store, helped Dad make the call. Meanwhile, Samaritans 3 and 4 stopped by and asked if they could help.

Samaritans 5 and 6 pulled up in their tow truck and, after a few valiant turns, declared the crushed lug nut unloosenable. "Only thing we can do is take you to a tire store and they can fix it for you Monday morning," they said.

Talk about a day going south fast. It's 5 p.m. Saturday, an icy breeze is blowing and we're 15 miles from our cabin. I'm focused on the present now, baby: How do we get back out there? How do we get back into town Monday morning? And what the heck are we gonna eat?

"There is no spot where God is not," my grandma used to say, and I always believed her. Just across the street was a bus with its engine running. Dial-a-ride, the towing guys called it. It's actually called Manistee County Transportation, the most wonderful public transport system in the world.

I walked over and asked if they could help us out. Driver Dave Hoffrichter, who was just about to get off work and take his wife to dinner, said no problem. He hauled us back out to our cabin in the woods, telling us about how he takes senior citizens shopping and high school kids skiing. For our $2 fare, he worked an hour overtime. Definitely Good Samaritan No. 7.

Add Joy Bass, the woman whose cabin we rented, as a big No. 8. Take my van to breakfast and dinner Sunday, back into town Monday and anywhere else you need to go, she said, throwing in two cans of soup and a loaf of bread.

On Monday morning, tire shop owner Phil Ludwigson (No. 9) took the crushed lug off and fixed our flat for 12 measly bucks.

So Dad and I got an extra day to re-connect, ski and loaf, thanks to our newfound friends. Suddenly, we were darn glad to have people around.

Feb. 3, 2001

Yellowstone rewards risk with beauty

A wide mouth in the ground gurgled up bubbles and steam. I stood and contemplated it, the sharp smell of sulfur scorching my nostrils. I suppose deep in my brain I considered the possibility that this pretty, simmering pool could explode and blast its scalding water all over me.

I looked out over a field of such gurgling wonders: deep blue-green hot springs rimmed with mustard-colored algae; black, yawning holes belching foul-smelling steam; castle-shaped geysers spewing clouds prior to their next spectacular eruption.

It was early evening in the Yellowstone geyser basin. But I felt like I was standing on Mars.

"It's an amazing place, isn't it?" a woman asked me as she walked by. Sure is, I agreed.

A monk strolled by, wrapped in a brown robe and carrying a staff. He nodded at me silently.

Steam rose up from countless fissures in the earth, like so many chimney pots venting strange underground hearths. Their eerie burbling was the only sound in the near-twilight. In distant forests and mountains all around me, elk grazed, wolves trotted, bears lumbered.

"Do not leave the paths," signs warned over and over again. The ground was uncertain here. Step toward one of those pretty pools, and you could fall through and be boiled.

The serenity I felt, gazing at the geyser basin's unearthly beauty, was tempered by my awareness of its hazards. This was an old volcano I was walking on. Stunning to look at, yes — and, potentially, deadly.

Beauty and danger: Constantly, on a two-week trip to the magnificent West, I was reminded of how inseparable these are in nature.

It was a theme reinforced often as I made my way mountainward on Int. 90, sharing a guys-only exploration of amazing America with my 12-year-old son and my brother-in-law. We hiked endlessly, drank all the pop we wanted and rarely washed our clothes.

But amid all the male bonding and lifelong memory-making, I kept feeling these little lessons being taught to me about the nature of creation. On calendars, it is merely beautiful. In experience, it is inherently risky — and rewards your risking.

The Grand Canyon of the Yellowstone took my breath away as I looked out over its awesome vista — then made my heart flutter when I glanced down at its 1,000-foot drop.

A climb to the top of 10,000-foot Mt. Washburn yielded fabulous views. But it took zero imagination to see how one false step could make me forever part of the scenery.

And no matter how noble the bison looked by the roadside, I knew they would not look so good if they suddenly charged their ton of muscle straight at me.

Beauty and danger. I felt them both at once after we climbed an enticing rock formation in the Badlands, then turned around to see a black storm approaching — fast.

This thrill of the risk, this catch of the breath on the awesome precipice is old hat to the rock climber, the sky-diver, the cave explorer. If you aren't a little scared, you aren't really experiencing nature. But nature is not a postcard; it is a powerful, unpredictable force that can make your spirit soar or dash your body against the rocks.

It didn't take too much hiking and climbing for me to get that this is the nature of experience itself. No venture — physical, intellectual or spiritual — rewards watching from a distance.

I have never gone very far or grown very much without doing things that made me a little scared. Speaking to a roomful of people; owning up to things of which I am ashamed; claiming a belief despite doubt: These are small mountains I have scaled.

The dangers are clear. Rejection, failure, damaging mistakes are the bruises inflicted by the uncertain exploration of experience. But the hike yields precious finds. Kind of like turning a bend to see a moose tending her calf.

July 15, 2000

Take me to the water

We are people of many faiths here in West Michigan. But in high summer, most of us go to the same place to nourish our spirits: the water.

It could be the Big Lake, crashing with breathtaking power, pushing back the surf boarders, buffeting the children like bobbing ducklings, turning their parents' feet blue with cold.

It could be one of 11,000 little to biggish lakes, rimmed with funky cottages and mossy docks, their lapping waves pungent with seaweed and fish and outboard motor oil.

It could be one of who knows how many rivers hurtling or meandering through our state, providing shade-dappled havens where people fish and glide by on canoes, rippling over rocks past tar-paper hunting cabins on bluffs.

Whether rippling, lapping or crashing, they all are life-giving waters. They quench our thirst, bathe our bodies and satisfy our souls.

Call them the baptismal font of our summer sanctuary. Michigan's lakes and rivers are holy waters. In them we are re-vitalized, born again if you will, whether by full immersion or simply dangling our toes.

We ought to sing a hymn to our waters.

"Shall we gather at the river (or lake) where bright angel (or little kids') feet have trod with its crystal tide forever flowing by the throne of God (or our beach chairs)?"

I have spent some time at the river (and lake) lately. This time of year, surely it is a sin not to. Forgive me, father, for I have not yet gotten sand in my toes.

They say in Michigan one is never more than 85 miles from a Great Lake or six miles from an inland lake. Where I live, Lake Michigan is half an hour by car, and the Grand River a mere bike ride away.

More than once, I have sensed God's spirit as I paused above the Grand on an old railroad bridge, watching kids cast their fishing lines from the sandy shore.

"On the margin of the river washing up its silver spray (and pop bottles) we will talk and worship ever (or pray for a bite) all the happy golden day (sometimes cloudy)."

Then there is that magic secret lake up north. I can't say its name. No matter, because there are thousands like it.

You've got your placid lake, your little burg with the ice-cream shop and general store. Fortunately few people know how magic it is or else it wouldn't be.

I recently spent a few days worshipping at my magic secret lake with old friends. We gather annually, staying at various cottages but always ending up at the beach. There, we read books, throw Frisbees, watch the sun set and start campfires.

Then we watch the stars appear, faintly at first, then filling the darkening sky with a bright sea of wonder. We gaze up and contemplate the awesome nature of creation.

Usually, the wonder eventually hushes our talking. Occasionally, we answer it gratefully with the soft strums of an acoustic guitar and a bravely rendered James Taylor tune drifting over the lake.

There is a rhythm to this, almost a kind of liturgy. Each day it comes around: the early morning walk, the aromatic breakfast, the midday beach hang, the gathering evening and the passed-around meal. There is community in it and, at heart, a quiet holiness.

Remember when Michigan license plates bore the motto "Water Wonderland"? That was back in the 1950s and '60s, when it seemed there would always be enough. Today, we wonder how much Great Lakes whitefish is safe to eat, and how to prevent distant states from sucking away our most precious resource.

It is more than wise to care for our waters — it is essential to our physical and spiritual well-being. They are holy and life-giving places where we gather, to play or to pray.

"Soon we'll reach the silver river (or crystal lake) soon our pilgrimage will cease (for at least a week); soon our happy hearts will quiver (and rest) with the melody of peace (or James Taylor)."

July 26, 2008

In praise of the everyday sacred

Set to verse by Frances deRoos Baron

Man at worship on beach,
           perfect late-summer day.
     If it were a painting,
         that could have been its title.
The man stood on the shore
           of Grand Haven State Park,
            gazing out at the water
               on a late afternoon.
    The sun glinted off his shades
         under a Ron Jon Surf Shop cap
            his shirt open to a strong breeze.
As we walked in front of him
        I heard him murmur,
           "So beautiful."
          I looked out to see the object of his awe.
       Ah, yes:
         his two little girls splashing
            in big, sunlight-flooded waves.
   So beautiful, indeed.
       I passed by quietly,
         feeling as if I'd intruded
            on a sacred moment.
A hymn would not have been out of place.
   Psalm 19 says it nicely:
    The heavens are telling the glory of God;
    and the firmament proclaims his handiwork.

Now there are those
   who would say the play of the daughters,

the power of the waves
and the glimmer of the sun were,
yes,
all glorious,
but not necessarily God's handiwork.
Maybe it's just natural selection
having a really good day.
I, on the other hand,
would say it was all
a bit too splendid for randomness.
I would throw in the father's softly exhaled praise
as evidence of a divinely instilled
recognition of the sublime.
But really, why debate the point?
Let's just agree it is sublime, and let me call it sacred.

In the waning weeks of a West Michigan summer
I can't think of a better word.
Because around here,
I see sacredness everywhere.
It could have been warmer.
You will not hear me complain.
It doesn't do to quibble much
about Michigan's moods.
If you'd rather live in Georgia,
no one is stopping you.

Me, I happily dwell in West Michigan,
where the sacred is more or less
an everyday experience.

Just look around at the beach:
See the grandparents wrapping towels
around their shivering grandkids;
the young buck carrying his sweetheart,
threshold-style,
into the surf;
the little girl chasing the seagulls into flight;
the older couple walking along the shore,
he dressed in a fine sport coat and fedora;

the mother taking Christmas card pictures
of her children at sunset.

And over it all,
the sun making its way
toward the glorious moment,
which a brave few of us stayed to behold,
when it sinks into the lake
with a parting flourish of gaudy brush-strokes.
Man, this must be what King David had in mind
with that Psalm.
There is no speech, nor are there words. . . Yet their voice goes out
through all the earth, and their words to the end of the world. The
sun comes forth like a bridegroom leaving his chamber, and like a
strong man runs its course with joy.

This voiceless speech by no means
is confined to the Lakeshore.
You hear it in the jammering kids
riding bikes down the block,
see it in the mighty oaks of John Ball Park,
taste it in that first lick of pistachio ice cream.

It is a kind of sacred backdrop we live in here
softening the harder edges of daily life:
the deadlines that wake you up;
the headlines that freak you out;
the SUV that roars up behind you like a Sherman tank.

When the stress of the normal
gets to be too much,
we do well simply
to be where we are
and look around.

Oh yeah, I almost forgot—
God's country.
Pretty nice handiwork.
The voiceless speech of late summer

inspires grateful reflection.
Call it what you will,
    sacred
      or survival of the sublime.
I think the father on the shore
        pretty well summed it up.
          So beautiful.

August. 29, 2009

Sixth Inning

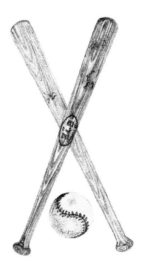

Bases Loaded

Goodbye Jetsons, hello millennium

Thank you for a new century.

That should be the prayer, mantra or transactional greeting for 70 million baby boomers as we rise and shine for the Big 21. We've finally grown up. And with everything we've seen and done, we're lucky just to be here.

Because for those of us who experienced reality as the last half of the 20th century, our prevalent view of the next millennium was cloudy at best. A mushroom cloud, to be exact. The future was potential annihilation. A world blown to smithereens. Planet Rubble.

Either that or an Earth where everyone loved each other and war was no more. You know, the Age of Aquarius.

This schizoid mind-set may not be unique to the JFK-Beatles-Vietnam generation, but we're sure the experts on it. I for one never had complete confidence that I would even see 2001. It was too easy to imagine some Dr. Strangelove lunatic pushing the red button. As for that other Stanley Kubrick classic, "2001: A Space Odyssey" looked colder and creepier than George and Jane Jetson's world.

Now that we're here, it's a little disorienting. Reassuring, but just too normal. No flying cars or nuclear winter. Just us, as always, and our usual problems. Still gotta get up in the morning, still gotta make ends meet, and still gotta figure out why we're here.

It's that last part that's moved a lot of us boomers into interesting spiritual territory. We grew up wanting to save the world, but found out the hard way we have to save ourselves. Now we're trying to save our kids, though from what we're not sure.

Many of us aren't even sure what being "saved" means. Eternal life? Freedom from fear? Freedom from mushroom clouds?

I grew up fearing those clouds, the grainy black-and-white H-bomb explosions I saw on TV and the chilling footage of Hiroshima being obliterated.

I'm not saying I thought about it while I was reading about Dick and Jane and Spot. But the mushroom cloud was always there in the back of my mind, like a ghost whispering, "Boom!"

Primal Bomb Fear began to fade a little during the '60s, eclipsed by the political bombshells going off right and left. If anything, hints of the apocalypse became more real as I watched blacks being attacked by German shepherds, Vietnamese peasants being napalmed and student protesters getting their heads bashed in.

Fortunately, there was this whole cultural euphoria thing going on that pretty much diverted me from the horror. I could deal with leftist radicals' predictions of a fascist takeover as long as the Beatles kept assuring me love was all I needed, and the Rolling Stones gave me a harmless way to vent my frustration.

The sum total of this war between light and darkness was a sense that the future probably was bleak, but that we could possibly change it all with the right combination of political action and artistic enlightenment.

The last place I looked for hope was the church, which in my experience had been something I sat through in mind-wrenching boredom or which produced Jesus freaks with that spooky light in their eyes. Even the counter-culturally respectable Eastern faiths turned out ambushing Hare Krishnas or suspect maharishis. Religion, I felt, was for those who couldn't handle the truth.

So it was with no small degree of wonderment that by the '80s I found myself willingly attending church services. Sure, I married into it. I wanted our kids to have spiritual underpinning. But I also went because I needed it. "Hi, I'm Charley and I'm a recovering agnostic."

There was no cinematic "a-ha" moment here, just a gradual realization that all my brains and friends and cool records weren't enough. They couldn't answer the challenges of work, marriage, child rearing and the hollowness inside. I sure wasn't getting my answers from the boomers, who'd morphed into the most materialistic, success-obsessed generation to ever stalk the earth.

So I turned inward, to walk the same lonely path people always have walked. I found plenty of fellow boomers on the way, amazed to find it was OK to talk about God. I'm walking it still, and a new millennium doesn't have that much to do with it.

It just tells me I'm lucky to still be here, with no mushroom clouds in sight.

Jan. 6, 2001

The dark without and the light within

I picked up the phone and heard my daughter's voice, brighter than the comfortless sunshine outside the office window. She told me she loved me. I told her I loved her, too.

That was all we had time for. I had to cover a noon Mass, where people prayed and wept for the thousands of people they knew had just died. And Emily went back to her studies at Western Michigan University.

Emily's call was the first contact I had with my family on Tuesday, Sept. 11. It was the first shaft of light that touched me, after the world became engulfed by a terrifying fireball and a hellish cloud of smoke.

Why is it that so many of us wanted to hear our children's voices, just touch their heads, after our national nightmare began shortly before 9 a.m. Tuesday?

Those who had children on the planes, in the towers or near them knew unbearable sorrow. Those of us who had them nearby still needed proof. Yes, they are still alive. Praise be to God.

As I worked dreamlike through the terrible hours, with a sick stomach, I kept thinking of my wife and children. The light of their presence shining in my mind was more palpable than the meaningless sunshine bathing a suddenly unreal landscape. My family was still there — at least that had not changed.

But the comfort I drew from that could not erase my fear, because I knew they were not safe. That much, at least, had been made abundantly clear.

And among all the overwhelming thoughts and feelings that raced through me, one kept coming back: We've failed them. We tried to prepare a better world for our kids, and we failed. I want to tell my children I'm sorry they had to see this much evil, that we couldn't stop it.

A few days later, I see some irrationality there. In many ways, our world is safer than in my youth. Polio is rare. I've seen no H-bomb tests lately.

All the same, the terrorists have cracked my confidence. I no longer know how safe or unsafe my children are. I don't know what the future holds for them, and that scares me.

Here's what else scares me: the people I have overheard today. Looks like World War III, one said. If we go down, we'll take the rest of the world with us. Someone called it all exciting, foreseeing, I gathered, a biblical end times in the making.

Wonderful. We're already thinking like the terrorists. Two eyes for one eye, with God on our side.

Today, I'm tired of the fear. I'm tired of this knot in my stomach, and I have my children to think about. There are things I want them to know.

I want them to know about the interfaith service Tuesday night at St. Andrew's Cathedral. Christians, Jews, Muslims and others packed the place, to praise their one God and defiantly declare their faith in the face of murdering monsters.

I want them to know about all the people giving blood, shipping supplies, offering their loving hands to anguished people half a country away, and that they are lucky to live in such a compassionate community.

I want them to know about all the prayers coming out of West Michigan, prayers of hope sent up from the rubble of grief.

I want them to know the wickedness done this week has nothing to do with any legitimate religion on earth, but only with a number of twisted souls seeking to anoint their evil with sacred oil.

I want them to know there are things we must and can do to reduce injustice and inequity, which do not justify evil but provide its breeding ground.

And I want them to know we can lick this evil. I don't know why I believe that. Maybe surviving the Cold War made me naively optimistic. But I believe we can rebuild our shattered reality and, with our children's help, make the world a far better place than it is this week.

Maybe I believe that because I can still see the light. It may be coming from far away, but it shines through the faces of the faithful, glows in the hands of the helping and radiates in the spirits of our children.

Long after the darkness clears, they will still be around, and I cannot help but believe they are the light of this world.

Sept. 15, 2001

'The heavens could explode any day'

Fat snowflakes fell on Rueben Allen's grizzled goatee and brown ski cap. Standing in line for lunch at God's Kitchen on South Division Avenue, he reckoned only God could create the snow, or the heat of summer for that matter. Therefore, there must be a heaven.

"It's going to be better," Allen said of the heavenly life. "You won't have no need. You won't want anything. You won't ever thirst again."

But he could not say for sure whether he, a middle-aged resident of the downtown YMCA, will taste the sweet waters of heaven. All he had to go on was Christ's sacrifice.

"There's a great possibility I will, 'cause he laid down his life for everyone," Allen said, as the lunch line moved along.

Ah, heaven. The devout praise it. Most Americans believe in it. "That would just be heaven," they say of getting that cottage on the lake. But what exactly is heaven like? Eden restored? Perfect, disembodied souls? A luxurious mansion? And will we remember earth if we get to heaven?

Most people agree we won't know for sure until we enter the pearly gates or some other luminous portal to the great beyond. But that heaven exists — all appearances on earth to the contrary — true believers are certain.

"I have no doubt about it," said JoAnne McKenzie in between fielding phone calls at United Methodist Community House, a ministry serving a struggling neighborhood south of downtown.

Asked if it is possible that life on earth is all there is, she protested, "Oh, heavens no!"

Despite such confidence in the hereafter, people's visions of it run the gamut from concrete Scriptural descriptions to gauzy New Age images.

Some invoke scenes from the book of Revelation; others from the movie "What Dreams May Come." Still others cite passages in "Life on the Other Side," Sylvia Browne's tour of the afterlife.

When it comes to heaven, it seems there are no experts.

Lyle Bierma, however, knows a lot about the doctrine of the end times, which he teaches as a systematic theology professor at Calvin Theological Seminary.

At Christ's second coming, all the believers throughout history take resurrected bodies and join the living for the eternal life on earth that God originally intended. People will live happily — and busily — in the full presence of God.

"We'll continue to write music, paint, build houses, farm," Bierma said. "There will be a lot to do. I hope to be playing tennis."

A walk through West Michigan shows that the beauty of heaven is in the eye of the believer.

As Rueben Allen ate at God's Kitchen, Program Manager Bobbi Britton sat in her office and painted a vivid picture of life after death.

"In my heaven, it's always warm," Britton said with assurance. "There are also animals. It's peopled by everyone you love. There always seems to be background music ... very ethereal kinds of stuff, harp music

"There's no concept of time, and there's nothing that one has to do," Britton said, writing notes as she talked. "There are no deadlines, and one eats to one's heart's content — chocolate, preferably."

She doubts there is a physical hell, but believes people move away from personal hells and closer to heaven by confronting their flaws in life. Everyone, Christian and otherwise, ends up in heaven, Britton believes.

And just where is that?

"I have no idea," she said, then thought better of it. "It's in God's imagination. That's as good a place as any."

Actually, it's right in front of us, Sister Geraldine Fox said.

"I think heaven is here, where we meet people," she said after morning Mass at Marywood with fellow Dominican sisters.

Supported by a cane, the tiny, smiling woman greeted aging nuns filing out of the chapel, where they received Communion and recited the Lord's Prayer with clasped hands.

Sister Geraldine saw heaven in her relationship with the beauty of the world and with the sisters walking by.

"God is here. God is in everybody. I don't care if you're Catholic or Muslim," she said, her blue eyes bright beneath snowy hair. "Heaven is also seeing God face to face, however you picture God."

A few miles south, Peter Berghoef sat in a Calvin College coffee shop, reading poetry and grappling with doubt.

A stack of books by E.E. Cummings, Ernest Hemingway and other authors lay before him. Berghoef, sporting a goatee, put away a notebook of his poetic explorations. One of them, "Jesus Rides a Pink Bike Through Every Scene," appeared in a college literary magazine:

"yes no maybe so - /what will we do? / the heavens could explode /any day now..."

"It's futile to try to imagine what sort of perfect existence it could be," said Berghoef, 21, an English student from Holland. "It has to be something truly different, truly great."

His visions of heaven are tinged with the Christian Reformed teachings of his childhood, a light and airy heaven where everyone is happy. They also are layered with images of C.S. Lewis, who portrayed a renewed Narnia in "The Last Battle."

"Heaven will be what earth was meant to be, before the fall — sort of unspoiled, everything good about this world," Berghoef speculated. "It would probably be a purer form of happiness than we would ever know in this life."

Probably. But he also wrestles with the possibility that no heaven or hell lies beyond this life. He has come to accept he cannot know for sure.

"Whether or not it exists, what Jesus had to say about the way people ought to treat each other is worth following," he said firmly. "I don't think the point was we do (things) so you go to heaven. You do them to create heaven on earth."

Farther west on Burton Street SE, Sharif Sahibzada thumbed through a Quran for descriptions of heaven. He found one in surah (chapter) 3, colorfully portraying the gardens awaiting those who fear the Lord:

"For the righteous are Gardens in nearness to their Lord with rivers flowing beneath; therein is their eternal home, with spouses purified and the good pleasure of Allah."

Other passages describe the faithful reclining on richly brocaded carpets, with chaste maidens near, precious stones, ever-flowing fountains, pomegranates and lofty mansions.

"Heaven and paradise, it's the same thing," said Sahibzada, spiritual leader of the Islamic Center and Mosque of Grand Rapids. "Oh, a joyful, happy place."

But even in luxurious paradise, the greatest happiness will be to stand before God.

"This world is going to finish," he said with certainty. "That world is forever."

At St. John Chrysostom Russian Orthodox Church, the world is shrunk to the size of a tiny, ornately decorated chapel. Early one day, the Rev. Andrew Keith Lowe lighted oil lamps and prayed in preparation for divine liturgy. On this snowy day, however, no worshippers came to the West Side church.

Colorful icons of Christ, Mary and the saints glowed from the walls and the smell of incense was strong, like prayers rising to heaven. Here, in the rich liturgy of angelic hymns and the mystical banquet of communion, the Orthodox believe heaven and earth meet.

As for heaven itself, Lowe imagines it might be something like the mountains west of Sydney in his native Australia.

"Being with God, in the rays of his light, it's like being in the sun on a beautiful spring day," Lowe said, sitting in the softly lighted church. "You're just soaking up that sunlight."

His heaven is a spiritual, not a physical, place. But it is no less real than his church, no less true than God.

"Jesus Christ by his death and resurrection has called us to a higher reality, a higher state. We're called to be God-like, and eventually be with God. That's what it means to be in heaven."

Back at God's Kitchen, Rueben Allen could envision a place without pain or sickness, run by a kind man named Jesus.

"One day, after I pass from this life," he said, "hopefully, he'll come and get me."

Jan. 26, 2002

Rob Bell's hell too velvet for some

A group of theologians last week decided the Rev. Rob Bell's hell just isn't horrible enough.

Albert Mohler, president of Southern Baptist Theological Seminary in Louisville, Ky., took a tongue-in-cheek shot at Bell's new book, "Love Wins," which argues the iron gates don't slam shut forever and God never gives up on anyone. Mohler quipped he thought of calling it "Velvet Hell" after Bell's first book, "Velvet Elvis."

Fellow Baptist theologian Denny Burk chimed in with stronger stuff, charging Bell removes God's wrath and downplays hell's terror.

"It is a horror that doesn't end," said Burk, dean of Boyce College, a division of SBTS. "There's no anesthetic, and you never settle in. And we all deserve it."

That'll scare the hell out of you, all right. But Burk said God showed his love by sending his son to the cross, and "used up all his anger that he had towards us on Jesus. ... You don't know the love of God if you don't know the wrath of God."

That conviction is one of the popular story lines to emerge in reaction to Bell's latest book, which has provoked both strong condemnation and admiration from evangelicals.

For many Christians, it seems, belief in the promise of heaven is inextricably tied to belief in everlasting hell. To pretend otherwise, as some Bell critics charge, is trying to make the gospel palatable to modern sensibilities at the expense of truth.

Commenters also have dug into the question that seems to bedevil many: Would a loving God condemn people to eternal suffering with no chance of release? Is hell life without parole for sinners?

To which I'll add: Is the answer about what Scripture says, or what seems right to us as humans?

Critics also berate Bell for presenting a God who can save souls through Jesus without their knowledge, so non-Christians potentially can get to heaven. You expect this kind of thing from liberal theologian John Shelby Spong, Mohler said, but coming from an evangelical like Bell, it may contribute to "loss of the gospel."

This is an absurd worry for anyone who has read Bell's books and heard his sermons. "Love Wins" is laced with Scripture, and its reference point is always Jesus.

"He holds the entire universe in his embrace," Bell writes. You don't need a flashlight to find the gospel there.

But Bell also rejects the traditional father-God who in one moment loves his children, and the next casts them into eternal agony.

"If there was an earthly father who was like that, we would call the authorities," he writes.

If there's one thing the Bell brouhaha points out, it is evangelicals don't all think alike. Far from it.

Richard Mouw, president of Fuller Theological Seminary, hardly a bastion of liberal theology, writes that Bell's views have roots in C.S. Lewis. Citing the evangelical view that only justification by faith admits believers to heaven, Mouw tells Christians "shame on you" if they believe Mother Teresa didn't make the cut.

"Why don't folks who criticize Rob Bell for wanting to let too many people in also go after people like that who want to keep too many people out?" writes Mouw, a former Calvin College professor.

Bell's is no voice in the wilderness. A 2007 Pew poll found 57 percent of evangelical Protestants believed other religions can lead to eternal life. So did 79 percent of Catholics and 83 percent of mainline Protestants. And while 82 percent of evangelicals believed in hell, only 59 percent of the general public did.

Of course, majority rule isn't necessarily correct. And there is a human logic to traditional views. Most of us see justice as life without parole or worse for murderers, rapists and child molesters. Shouldn't God see it the same way?

Certainly, if God were like us. But Bell is hardly the first theologian to say God is not like us. He quotes the Old Testament book of Lamentations, chapter 3: "People are not cast off by the Lord forever."

That's pretty hard for the average person to believe, especially if his own father cast him off forever. Maybe God is more like the father who welcomes his wayward, prodigal son back home with open arms.

Ultimately, these are questions of mystery, their answers unknowable this side of the grave.

Meanwhile, the hells on earth are clear enough. From these people certainly can be saved.

March 26, 2011

Let's get rid of those messy humans

I am getting comfortable with buying groceries from a machine.

Not that I have much choice. Pretty much any grocery store I walk into anymore wants me to pay for my 12 or fewer items at an automated cashier.

I feel some guilt about putting actual human cashiers out of work. But maybe I'm sparing them the stress of constantly serving people by going to the machine and obeying the nice female machine voice:

"Please place your item in the bag. Please select payment method. Please insert coins, then insert bills. Please remember to take your receipt."

The female machine voice is invariably efficient and polite. She doesn't have any disagreeable warts on her face — doesn't have a face at all, in fact — and doesn't cough into her hand before giving me change.

And she doesn't engage me in pointless conversation that will make me late for getting home and flopping down in my easy chair.

The automated grocery cashier represents a welcome evolution in society, in my view. It makes buying food a cleaner, less troublesome transaction.

And it frees employees from the tiresome task of ringing up orders so they can, well, do other jobs, or something.

I realize most cashiers enjoy helping people buy food and sending them on their way with a smile. But isn't that awfully old-fashioned in the automation age?

This encouraging trend was started by gas stations. Thank heaven we no longer have those guys with silly uniforms hovering around our autos, filling the gas tank, cleaning the windshield and checking the oil. What pests!

Now, we can just fill our own darn tanks, clean our own windshields, pay at the pump and drive away with that manly smell of gas on our hands.

Lately, I noticed this trend has made its way into movie theaters. Instead of standing in line to buy tickets from some annoying young adult with a pierced eyebrow, we can stand in line to buy them from a perfectly polite machine. Again, more efficiency, and no possibility of germs coming with the ticket.

Given the great success of automation in the business world, I am thinking churches have something to learn here.

After all, isn't it the modern church's mission to be non-threatening? To make worshippers feel casual and comfortable? To "meet people where they are," in church planters' parlance?

Certainly one of the least comfortable church rituals has to be communion. Taking the wafer or breaking off a chunk of bread from the pastor, sipping the wine from a thimble cup or (shudder) a common chalice — it's positively icky human interaction rife with the possibility of embarrassing accidents, not to mention outright contamination.

I think a communion-dispenser machine is an idea whose time has come. No chance for embarrassment with the helpful female-machine voice to guide you:

"Please eat the wafer. Please sip the wine. Please recycle the plastic cup. Please don't forget to take the peace of God with you."

Computers could also make worship more user-friendly. T.D. Jakes' church in Dallas outfits pews with data ports so worshippers can download sermon notes on their laptops. Let's take this to the next level.

In the information age, worshippers should be able to choose from a menu of sermons. No one should have to endure half an hour of preaching on a boring subject. Don't like Pastor VanderVeen's sermon on Job? Click on "sermon surf" and go to Robert Schuller expounding on the prodigal son.

Same with hymns. The Internet has shown the power of downloading music. Why not download "Jesus, Hold Me Close" if you don't want to hear "Be Thou My Vision"? Equip every pew station with headphones, and you're all set.

As for all those hugs while "passing of the peace" — yuck. Just text-message "peace be with you" to everyone, then get back to your downloading.

These improvements would make worship more modern, efficient and, ultimately, safer. And isn't that what we all want?

Because human beings, God love 'em, can just be such a nuisance.

Sept. 18, 2004

The Amish touch us with forgiveness

Late afternoon on the day of Kathryn Miller's funeral, a sense of peace surrounded her parents' Fremont farmhouse where Amish from far and wide had come to comfort them.

Little girls in long black dresses and white bonnets bounced up and down on a trampoline. Boys pushed themselves along on scooter-like bicycles. Dozens of men and women in plain dark clothes talked contentedly over plates of ham sandwiches and jello.

Orlie Miller looked up from his plate and calmly explained why he harbored no resentment against Mark Vandyke, the Fremont man who allegedly killed 11-year-old Kathryn on Sunday night. Police say Vandyke was intoxicated when he drove his truck into the Miller family buggy as they returned from a hymn sing.

"We hold nothing against anybody," said Miller, who is not related to the family. "If Christ was able to forgive those who nailed him to the tree, we can't do any less."

Sitting next to him, Leon Coblentz was equally eloquent as he spoke of Christ's call to turn the other cheek.

"If we're going to get resentful and hate him, we're not going to be any better off than he is," Coblentz said.

Their words sounded as right as Scripture, as natural as the mooing of a nearby cow — and astonishing in their simple forgiveness.

It was the same spirit we heard emanating from Lancaster County, Pa., where earlier this month a gunman murdered Amish schoolgirls. While the rest of us felt outrage, the Amish comforted the murderer's family and turned out at his funeral.

Kathryn's tragic death this week brought amazing Amish grace close to home.

They stand quietly at the edge of society, working their fields and selling us pies. They ask little but to live and worship as they choose. And as our world has burst violently into theirs, they have taught us something profound.

The Amish point us in a direction we are not used to looking: toward total acceptance, total forgiveness, total trust in God.

It is not a lesson to make us disconnect our phones and don dark clothes. But it is precious insight into how we live and could live.

Consumed with control, trying to make everything turn out right, fearful of its going wrong, doubting God's goodness: These go hand-in-hand with American life. They certainly are demons that devil me daily.

In accepting tragedy, submitting fully to God and truly living forgiveness, the Amish breathe wisdom into our harried world. They express a peace with life that comes from peace with God.

Peace is what you feel in the Amish country around Fremont. You look around at the blazing yellow maples, the sun shimmering on corn and water and you think, no wonder they want to live here.

I felt like an intruder in this world as I walked into Levi Ray and Amelia Miller's yard, which earlier that day had hosted hundreds of Amish from around the Midwest.

As he finished dinner, Orlie Miller patiently explained how his faith works in Kathryn's death. He spoke of Paul's teaching that all things work together for good in God.

"We're either spreading love and forgiveness or we're spreading hate and bitterness," he said. "There's too many people in this world who are halfway in between."

He expressed sympathy for Vandyke's parents and said there was talk among the Amish of visiting them.

As for Kathryn, Leon Coblentz took comfort in his sure knowledge she is in heaven.

On the way to the hymn sing Sunday night, he said, Kathryn asked her parents to sing "I Have Decided to Follow Jesus."

"That's very encouraging for us to know that."

Oct. 28, 2006

Gay and Christian: courage under fire

A firefight on the road to Baghdad helped give Daniel Dobson the courage to come out as a gay man.

Dobson, then 18, had been in Iraq only a few weeks when his U.S. Army gun truck came under heavy fire from al Qaeda. He froze up momentarily with fear. But he reached deep in his gut to withstand the assault, helped by a note card he'd put on the windshield. It quoted the book of Hebrews:

"The Lord has said, 'Never will I leave you; never will I forsake you.' So we say with confidence, 'The Lord is my helper, I will not be afraid. What can man do to me?'"

The verse had been given to him by his father, the Rev. Ed Dobson, who had turned to it often in his battle with Lou Gehrig's disease.

While that 2004 attack was terrifying, it helped prepare Daniel for an even scarier moment almost two years ago. He stood outside his parents' door and repeated Hebrews 13:5-6 to himself. Then he told them, "Mom, dad, I'm gay. And I still love Jesus. And nothing else changes."

After a stunned silence, he recalls, his father said, "We still love you. And nothing else changes."

The relief of hearing that was "absolutely huge," says Dobson, now 28. "It almost felt like I was able to breathe again."

It had taken him 13 years to divulge his sexual orientation to his parents. Today, Dobson feels ready to tell the rest of us.

It's another scary step, he admits, especially for the younger son of Ed Dobson. The retired pastor of Calvary Church is one of West Michigan's most prominent ministers and a former top aide to the late Jerry Falwell, founder of the Moral Majority. Who knows how people will react?

Whatever the reaction, speaking out is the right thing to do, says Daniel, a recent film studies graduate of Cornerstone University.

"It's morally right for me to do it," Daniel Dobson tells me at a Grand Rapids cafe. "I feel I have something good to contribute to the conversation, something positive."

He wants people to know it is possible to be gay and a faithful Christian. The Bible passages often cited to condemn homosexuality don't apply to two men or two women loving each other or gay marriage, Dobson argues.

"A lot of gays and lesbians are hurting because they don't know it's OK," he adds.

Others also will offer alternative biblical perspectives in a panel discussion at Wealthy Theatre. The event was organized by Matthew Clark, a psychologist at Human Resource Associates. Clark, who is gay and Christian, says he regularly sees clients who struggle to reconcile their faith with what they have been told about what the Bible says.

"They've heard it's a sin to be gay and that they're going to burn in hell for it," Clark says.

Clark offers them different views of biblical texts he says are widely misinterpreted. For many, it is a healing revelation.

"They get a huge burden taken off them," Clark says. "They're no longer feeling suicidal and depressed."

Clark's program follows the Boy Scouts' decision to allow gay members and the coming out of pro athletes Jason Collins and Robbie Rogers. As in those cases, Daniel Dobson's coming out will engender both praise and dismay.

But for Dobson, it's a matter of personal integrity and biblical imperative.

He says he knew he was gay at age 13 but never acted on it. That seemed the wisest choice growing up in a conservative, evangelical world.

"I was thinking if I even talk about this I'm going to be ostracized, lose all my friends. For a long time, I prayed I wouldn't be gay."

He kept his orientation to himself after enlisting in the Army, where he served two tours in Iraq. He loved the military — he is still a specialist in the Army Reserve — and did not want to jeopardize his ability to serve under the Army's "don't ask, don't tell" policy then in force.

However, a near-engagement with a girl convinced him he could not live a lie. He questioned why God would make him gay and then damn him for it. But as he looked closer at the Bible, he found nothing condemning same-sex relationships between adults in the modern sense.

He finally resolved to tell his parents, Ed and Lorna, calling on the courage of combat and the assurance of God's love.

"It came down to a matter of personal integrity for me, that I had to be honest with myself and with the world," Dobson says.

He has learned much about integrity from seeing his father endure criticism for unpopular stands, and from hearing his mother quote biblical imperatives to do right. He also wrestled through Scripture with his brother, Kent, pastor of Mars Hill Bible Church.

All this leads him to believe it's time to speak out, both to help needlessly suffering people and to counter hateful Christian attitudes toward gays.

"Because of what Christians say about gays and lesbians, they don't get to share Jesus at all. They hurt the kingdom and they hurt Jesus. What they're saying cannot possibly be led by the (Holy) Spirit."

I've long admired the courage of Ed Dobson. Daniel's decision shows the same character. I hope even those who disagree with his theology will respect his integrity.

May 29, 2013

Transformed by St. Francis, in Assisi

If there's a place God's going to break through, the Basilica of St. Francis is a promising venue.

There, flanked by huge Giotto frescoes depicting the 13th-century saint's life, I listened rapt as the basilica choir sang Rutter's "The Lord Bless You and Keep You." By the final "amen," I was pretty sure God was touching my neck right where it makes the hairs stand up.

It wasn't the first nor the last time I felt rapt and wrapped by a divine presence during a recent week in Assisi, Italy. Not so much jaw-dropping as heart-cradling, the five-day sojourn in Francis' birthplace brought home the power of faith and love to span centuries and continents.

I was drawn to Assisi by a remarkable event called "A Global Gathering: The Pilgrimage of Love and Forgiveness." It was put on by the Fetzer Institute, a Kalamazoo-based foundation that works to highlight those values through research, media and demonstration projects.

The gathering itself was reason enough to sense a transcending love at work through the muck and mayhem of this sorry world. About 550 leaders of humanitarian efforts, many but by no means all of them faith-based, came together to share their experiences serving some of the world's most God-forsaken areas. I wrote about the results in a story for Religion News Service.

Fetzer's organizers knew what they were doing when they chose Assisi as the site. Set high in the hills of Umbria, home to Grand Rapids' sister city of Perugia, Assisi is what they call a thin place, nearer to the spiritual plane than your average burg. It is a popular pilgrimage destination, attracting some six million visitors a year for its breathtaking art, winding medieval streets and the enduring spirit of St. Francis.

"Assisi is a place that has vibrations, spiritual vibrations," Bhai Sahib Mohinder Singh, a Sikh leader from Birmingham, England, told me. "It doesn't matter what religion or continent you belong to. You are drawn toward Assisi."

Artist Mic Carlson is among many West Michigan folks who have been so drawn. Carlson felt Francis kidnap his heart during a 1995 visit, spurring him to create a series of sculptures of the saint. One of them is housed at the Basilica of St. Francis; others grace a meditation garden at the Marywood home of the Grand Rapids Dominican sisters.

Carlson and others had told me Assisi would be a life-changing place. Still, I wasn't prepared for its spiritual impact despite a bad head cold and serious jet lag.

"The sense of peace is profound," I wrote in the middle of one restless night, looking out my hotel window over quiet streets and a picturesque abbey. "This place gives me a feeling of over-whelming love and acceptance, God loving me just as I am."

One could just as well feel that in, say, Holland as in Assisi, a town of similar size though considerably older. There's no telling where a sense of the divine will touch down like a dove or a Hindu goddess. It has at least as much to do with the spiritual state of the person as the geographic place.

But Assisi has built-in advantages for spiritual awakening. Days begin and end to the sound of church bells. Laughter and song echo through its steep, narrow alleyways. It is riddled with churches and convents, where you can randomly come upon nuns singing in an ancient chapel.

I even found divine sustenance in the little cafe just up the road from my hotel, where each morning the gracious cafe own-er made me delicious and artfully decorated cups of cappucci-no. For us, a simple "grazie" sufficed.

The sense of grace was enhanced, however, by the Global Gathering. It was a kind of coming-out for the Fetzer Institute, which has stayed below the radar for nearly 25 years while funding such notable efforts as the "God in America" series on PBS. Fetzer's founder was the late John Fetzer, media magnate and Detroit Tigers owner, who called love "the core energy that rules everything."

Fetzer's belief in connecting inner spirit to outer service was well represented in Assisi. From bereaved Israeli and Palestinian parents seeking reconciliation, to yoga as healing for rape victims, and music as therapy for hospice patients, participants presented powerful ways to heal and repair the world.

I'd gone to this summit with my brother, Mike, expecting signs of hope. These I saw in abundance. But I wasn't prepared for the personal transformation wrought by the power of healing hands across continents, and the spirit of St. Francis across time.

I felt it fully on the gathering's final night when, in a concert next to the basilica, we heard Italian tenor Andrea Bocelli sing "Ave Maria." From the gifted voice of a blind singer, back through the exquisite melody of Schubert, to the life of the saint entombed under the basilica, and back again through a song my mother loved, God's voice rang clear as a church bell.

Oct. 11, 2012

Give peace a chance, in your heart

I Googled "peace": 253 million hits. Impressive.

I Googled "war": 800 million hits.

Wait a minute — peace, 253 million; war, 800 million?

What is Google, the all-seeing oracle of our age, telling us? Google looks at our culture and reports back three times more references to war than to peace.

That's either a whole lot of fighting or a ton of video games.

Let's try the dictionary.

"Peace: the normal freedom from civil commotion and violence in a community ... silence, stillness."

Wait a minute. Silence and stillness: check. But "normal"? Peace is "normal"?

It sure doesn't feel normal. We are so rarely at peace, in our world or in our hearts.

Yet peace is the normal we long for and work for and believe in with all we've got.

It is the wish Christian worshippers exchange with handshakes and hugs: "Peace be with you."

It is the sacred salutation of Muslims: "Peace be upon you." It is the welcoming "shalom" of Jews and the respectful "namaste" of Hindus and Buddhists.

And it is the fervent wish, "All we are saying is give peace a chance," found in the gospel of John. Lennon.

In our very language, we acknowledge the rightness of peace. We try to bring it into being and make it normal. Yet is seems so difficult to achieve.

How can we expect peace in the world when it is so lacking in our hearts?

Peace comes to most of us in random moments — a splendid sunset, a beautiful song or the stillness and silence of meditative prayer.

We seek it behind the din of an always-talking world: the babble of cell phones and TV talking heads, the roar of highways and explosions of roadside bombs.

We find it in a breeze stirring up leaves on a street lined with fine maples, or the calm demeanor of an elder serenely waiting on death. At such times, we feel peace is the natural order.

I have felt it many times, whether pushing my daughter on the swing, playing catch with my son or murmuring the Lord's prayer with my congregation. It lasts just a few minutes, then slips away, chased off by the worries and fears of that day's headlines and bills.

Trouble, worry and fear — sometimes that seems the natural order of things.

How can we be at peace when our country is at war, abroad and at home? Sons and daughters, mothers and fathers are fighting in Afghanistan. The airwaves are awash in the rancor that fuels ratings, and neighbors yell at each other over, um, health care.

Ours is a shouting culture, and what it shouts is: "Be very afraid! Don't trust anyone! They're out to get you! Hang on to what is yours, and, for God's sake, don't pay more taxes!"

No wonder Google sees a lot more war than peace.

It seems peace and war are always vying for our hearts, like two brothers wrestling in the dirt. Sometimes it's hard to tell them apart, as if they are two aspects of the same struggle.

Yet we know in our hearts that peace is our proper condition. It's how we are meant to live. It's what we were created for.

It speaks to us across millennia in the Bible: "The Lord bless you and keep you; the Lord make his face shine upon you ... The Lord turn his face toward you and give you peace."

Whatever your belief system, these words ring true. We sense they are meant for us. We believe in our hearts we are a people of peace.

I think we can trust our hearts. It is the one place Google can't see.

Oct. 10, 2009

Seventh Inning

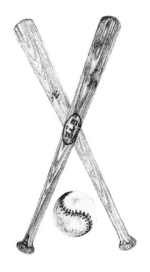

Waiting on Deck

Are you there, God? It's me, Charley

I envy Neale Donald Walsch's access to God.

Walsch wrote the best-selling "Conversations with God," an extended account of his purported dialogue with the Almighty. God carries on with him about the power of love, why everyone gets to heaven and, I suppose, how to improve your bowling score.

Walsch has even had follow-up conversations with God, worth two more books.

The dude obviously has a way with God that I don't. My typical conversation with God goes like this:

ME: Hello, God. I am having some tough issues in my life lately and could use your help. What should I do to be happier and less stressed?

GOD:

ME: Let me put it this way. What is your will as to how I should live my life?

GOD:

ME: OK, I can see you have a lot going on. Let me get back to you on this. It's been nice talking toward you.

I am not saying God never responds to my prayers. But generally he is pretty stingy with his advice, especially compared with how much God talked to people in the Bible. He practically yaks Moses' leg off and tells everyone what to eat, who to attack and how to build boats.

But I ask him one simple thing — Should I do this or not? — and get back dead air. Maybe if I led a people out of exile, he'd pay more attention to me.

Finding God more reticent than usual lately, I went to a guy who is familiar with the Lord's maddening silences. As Calvin College chaplain since 1979, Dale Cooper has counseled many a student having trouble getting through to God.

One came to his office the other day, deeply distraught. She told Cooper, "I need answers. I don't know where or how to get them. What can you reasonably expect out of God?"

Cooper often asks himself the same question. He expects a lot, but there are times when God just doesn't answer. Cooper figures he is either not ready to hear it or is not listening closely enough.

He recalls David's agony in Psalm 13: "How long, O Lord? Will you forget me forever?"

"I think God longs to speak to human beings," says Cooper, who is unfailingly cheerful and able to call up Scripture at will. "The problem is, I live in life with all its complications. The static in my life is often so intense that I'm either unable or unwilling to know how to listen."

He tries to begin all his prayers by listening. Then, he talks to God. Even if God does not answer, Cooper never doubts he is listening, like a loving parent or spouse.

I wish I had his faith. When God gives me the silent treatment, I'm like, "OK, I see how you are. You are just too big for me. For you, the problems of one little person don't amount to a hill of beans in this crazy world. I'm sorry; am I bothering you?"

Not Cooper. But he has a powerful example to go by: his mother.

He watched as Marjorie Cooper was stricken with polio at age 26 and spent the last 40 years of her life in an iron lung.

"She died never having had her original prayer answered: 'Lord, make me well,'" Cooper says.

But what she did hear God say, eventually, is not to look back and say "if only" nor look forward and ask "what if?" In return, he promised never to forsake her.

She passed away, Cooper says, with Psalm 16 on her lips: "Therefore my heart is glad and my tongue rejoices ... because you will not abandon me to the grave."

God always answers, Cooper believes. It may not be immediately, or even with words. It may be through Scripture. Or through the example of faithful people or the loving concern of friends.

Sometimes, Cooper says, "You just have to say, 'Let others of us pray for you, and maybe you can return the favor sometime.'"

This all sounds very difficult to me. I want a God who says "yes," "no" or "try again later." But this does not seem to be the kind of God he is.

So I guess I'll just keep trying and have faith he is listening. And cares. And will answer, eventually.

Meanwhile, maybe I'll write a book: "Attempted Conversations With God."

Nov. 15, 2003

Guy power meets higher power

The quest for spiritual connection among men can be a tough trek.

Think of Billy Crystal and friends in "City Slickers." Think of Frodo and Co. in "The Lord of the Rings." Think of John Belushi and fellow frat brothers in "Animal House."

Any guy who's ever tried to get past "How about those Red Wings?" over a Bud Light knows it's easier to duct tape a cracked side-view mirror than to bond with another man.

There's just too much stuff in the way. Pride. Self-protection. Vulnerability. That one humiliating day in the junior-high locker room.

So, then, how about those Wings? Cheers, buddy.

Sometimes, however, a brew and the Wings are exactly where the quest starts, eventually leading you to places wondrous and dangerous.

Thus it was that six guys, myself included, found themselves stranded on Int. 75 on Sunday. The road was sheer ice, the wind kicked up blinding blasts of snow and ambulances rolled by on either side.

This backup south of Gaylord pushed us back to the North, back into the cozy cabin where we had just spent two days. Back to the woods, back to the primeval fire, back to the books, songs, food, drink and long, winding talks.

Oh darn.

This good gathering of guys began long ago and far away in a cabin of a different sort: a Grand Rapids alehouse known as Founders where, weekly for several years, our small group met to appreciate fine beer, the writings of Jim Harrison and one another's company.

I joined the company a couple of years ago. It has been a reliable pleasure ever since.

The group shrinks and swells as members move away, move back or move in. We span generations and vocations: a therapist/retired minister, his actor/writer son, a counselor to American Indians, an artist, a maverick, a fellow reporter and various guest stars.

We throw on the table anything that goes with beer and peanuts (which is everything): politics, relationships, theology, philosophy, sports and the social history of India pale ale.

From the trust and fellowship of that table grew the trip north to a 1912-built cabin overlooking the village of Wolverine, south of Burt Lake in Cheboygan County. Through its wide window Saturday night, we watched the winter storm gathering in horizontal sheets.

Pleasantly spent by cross-country skiing and snowshoeing, we fed the fire and savored God's good gifts: a delicious risotto, a smattering of ales and the magic of a Galway Kinnell poem read by Ron, owner of this monastic retreat.

"Half my life belongs to the wild darkness," Ron read as the winter wind exerted its icy mastery.

His son, Calin, sang Bob Dylan and other balladeers while I played guitar. Dan the artist recorded the proceedings on tape and camera, capturing dishes of food and snow-laden pines in equally loving detail.

Somewhere here, among the fire and food and thoughtful pauses between words, a rich spiritual connection quietly worked its way in. Our innate guy defenses were no match for its subtle power.

Just by being here, cooking and talking and laughing, we were forming bonds that we would never try to name, but which we knew would be there the next time we grasped each other's hands with a grin.

What is the connection? Beats me. But it has something to do with delight in sensory substances: the aroma of pasta sauce, the taste of pale ale, the cadence of a spoken poem.

It also has to do with the wild darkness and wind that howled outside and that which beat in our hearts.

In this trusted company of men, it was good to venture into both and dry off by the fire.

Feb. 16, 2008

Memory, where did I put you?

Somewhere out there is a pair of glasses looking for a home. That home would be mine, incidentally.

I lost them a few months ago, somewhere between the Gaslight Village D&W parking lot and Derby Station, where I had gone to meet friends. I definitely had the glasses when I drove to the parking lot, and definitely didn't when it came time to order.

No amount of retracing my steps, checking with the staff or Googling "Charley's glasses" has turned them up. I have been forced to accept my glasses are gone and release them to the universe, where no doubt they are orbiting in a kind of asteroid belt filled with All Things Lost on Earth: keys, wallets, single socks, very important computer files.

Probably 70 percent of these things were lost by people my age, baby boomers who once dreamed of saving the world but now routinely lock themselves out of their cars. Our revolutionary slogan, "Make Love, Not War," has been replaced by "Turn Off Coffee Pot."

I wonder if all my Woodstock cohorts keep getting the same email I do from Johns Hopkins University, labeled "Protect Your Memory as You Age." Every so often, it shows up in my inbox, which always makes me wonder, "Why are they sending this to ME? How do they know I put sticky notes on my fridge saying, 'You came in here for a reason?'"

These emails are not comforting: "If you're over 40, and you haven't noticed a change in your mental alertness and memory, you — unfortunately — may sooner than you think." Oh, thanks. May I also look forward to involuntarily burping at dinner parties? Don't answer that.

This cheerful missive goes on to explain that our ability to recall names, dates and figures fades as we move through our

50s, 60s and 70s. They ask, has this ever happened to you? Forget a friend's phone number, call people by the wrong name, can't think of the right word when talking?

I suppose "Every single day" is not a promising answer.

"Hey, man, how's it going?" really means, "Hey, person I've seen a million times, suddenly I can't remember your name!"

But Johns Hopkins promises all kinds of help in its memory white paper, which purports to reveal how the latest research can help you remember stuff and "retain what you read in newspapers, magazines and books."

Hopefully, it also can help us retain movie plots.

The white paper further promises to "help keep Alzheimer's disease at bay." Of course, the lurking fear among the increasingly forgetful is that we are among the 5.3 million with Alzheimer's — a tragic disease that is nothing to laugh at.

But how do we know whether we have dementia or just normal aging memory loss, or whatever you call it?

I attempted to find out awhile ago by taking a standardized memory test. It consisted partly of a woman giving me long lists of words, then my trying to repeat them. Being a reporter, I quickly figured out how to categorize the words to make them easier to remember. My proctor doctor gave me several runs at the list, and I felt a little less dense each time.

To my astonishment, I placed in the 98th percentile of good memory nationally. Or maybe it was the 92nd, I can't remember for sure. That made me feel better for a bit. But then I thought, what if I'm just good at recalling lists? I still can't find my glasses.

Just the other day, it was the keys. I was visiting my dad in the hospital when they disappeared. They remained missing overnight while I made an inventory of everywhere I had gone that day, detective Poirot-like.

The next morning, they were on my dad's tray table. I think the angels were just having a little fun with me.

Can faith help memory? "Remember your Creator in the days of your youth," says the scribe of Ecclesiastes. OK, but what about the days of my midlife?

Many people memorize Bible verses; a Muslim hafiz recites the entire Quran. Surely, I can remember to take the garbage out Thursday night.

In a recent blog on Guideposts, Executive Editor Rick Hamlin wrote he uses prayer to improve his memory. He looks at his notes of people to pray for, closes his eyes and recalls as many of them as he can.

"I've found with time that my memory gets better, and each new name I add is a chance to both expand my spiritual horizons and jog my mind," Hamlin writes.

Sounds good. I just have to put a sticky note on the fridge saying, "Don't forget to pray."

Sept. 24, 2011

Freaking out at the end of all things

The biggest news of the century, and it's probably lining someone's bird cage.

There it was, on the bottom of Page A3, scrunched beneath stories on North Korea and India Hindus trashing Valentine's Day: "NASA picture shines new light on beginning of universe."

Sounds innocent enough, huh? Read on. This pretty, simulated image showing the universe as a baby — just 380,000 years after it was born — contains dark news for all of us.

Dark energy, to be exact. According to a NASA space probe, 96 percent of the universe comprises dark energy and dark matter — and scientists don't even know what that is.

Only 4 percent is material things made up of electromagnetic atoms and known forces such as gravity. This includes the living, breathing beings we have all come to know and love — us.

This new picture of the universe, formed by measuring the microwave background radiation that causes snow on your TV screen, paints a bleak picture of the future.

Propelled by the Big Bang, everything will just keep moving farther from everything else. It will not, as I always hoped, eventually retract into the size of a shooter marble and blow back up again. It will just keep going until, eventually, everything is cold and dead.

It will all "peter out," is how one helpful scientist put it. "If you had to choose how the universe would end, by fire or ice, this is the ice answer."

Wonderful. Quintillions of babies born, diseases cured, Valentine poems written and "Cheers" episoides broadcast, and it all ends in ice.

And the scientists were thrilled with their discovery. Thrilled!

I guess it also would be thrilling to crash a party and tell all the guests an asteroid was headed their way.

I, on the other hand, am blown away.

Is no one else freaked out by this news? I found only one colleague who shares my angst. Everyone else was like, "Well, yeah, but that's, what, 10 billion years away? So who cares?"

Me! I care! This means the ultimate end of everything is nothing. It means Shakespeare had it right when he wrote, "Life's but a walking shadow. ... It is a tale told by an idiot, full of sound and fury, signifying nothing."

This revelation also puts in more poignant perspective God's bad news to Adam: "For dust you are and to dust you will return." Perhaps he was talking about cosmic dust.

Maybe I'm overreacting. It's not like we've never heard that the universe will wind down to nothing. But these NASA people seem so certain now, calling their findings "truly profound."

What profound meaning, then, does a cold, dead universe have for the religious traditions of the world, with their promises of eternal life, nirvana, reincarnation or final reunion with the godhead?

What of Revelation's new heaven and new earth, where believers will live forever in the presence of God?

What of God, the beginning and ending of all things, to whom belongs the kingdom and the power and glory, forever?

For those who think science has it all wrong, the dark-energy scenario poses no greater problem than the apparent contradictions between evolution and Genesis. But for those who take science and faith seriously, this is reason to draw in the breath.

It suggests, at least, a possibly profound disjuncture between physical and spiritual reality. Perhaps promises of the soul's eternal life don't hinge on planets or stars but exist on some other plane we can't comprehend. Or maybe, the very idea of eternity is bounded by physical realities we can't fathom.

Then again, if the universe is a one-shot deal, what does that imply about God's omnipotence? When the last ember burns out, will he be able to say, "You know, I think I can do better than that"?

I'll tell you this: With that much dark energy out there, I'm not wasting a minute worrying about the end. I'm going to fill every day of my 4 percent and hope the bright energy spreads.

Feb. 15, 2003

Chasing rainbows with Coltrane

The man was looking up and snapping something with his cell phone. I looked up, too, coming out of Family Fare with two bags full, and smiled: an exquisite rainbow.

It was remarkably distinct, fully spanning the eastern sky from north to south. Others were looking up now as I walked toward the car. It could have been a spaceship landing, the way they were craning their necks. I snapped a couple of my own, knowing how inadequately the pictures would represent this everyday miracle.

Suddenly everything seemed extra vivid, quickened, almost cinematic. I got in the car and punched on the radio. WGVU-FM was playing a jazz-jam version of "My Favorite Things" by John Coltrane, with McCoy Tyner on piano.

They turned the tune into a meandering journey as I turned left onto Lake Michigan Drive, the lyrics faintly echoing from my childhood memory:

Raindrops on roses and whiskers on kittens
Bright copper kettles and warm woolen mittens
Brown paper packages tied up with strings
These are a few of my favorite things ...

Driving east, I was headed straight toward the magnificent rainbow. It looked like I could drive right under it, as if it were the St. Louis Gateway Arch. Maybe I could. I kept driving toward downtown, driven by the tumbling Coltrane jam, pulled by the splendid prism.

In the book of Genesis, God sets a rainbow in the clouds as a covenant between himself and Noah, all his descendants and the earth for all time. No more floods destroying everything, ever again.

"Whenever the rainbow appears in the clouds, I will see it and remember the everlasting covenant," God tells Noah.

So, we like rainbows. They impart hope, beauty, wonder. You never know when they'll come, and when they do they remind you how beautiful the world is. Born out of the blue quite suddenly, and then gone. They are one of the few things that still make us gasp with delight.

One of our favorite things: God splashing a paint brush across the sky.

I kept pursuing the perfect arch, straight east now, the J.W. Marriott breaking the skyline right in front of me. Coltrane's sax played crazily like a man running up and down hills. The rainbow was almost straight overhead, but it was fading into the clouds. Its northern arc glimmered a moment longer, then it too was gone.

I turned around and drove home, at peace. I had glimpsed glory for all of 10 minutes. That's more than you can ask for most days.

Soulmailing, May 4, 2012

Paddling down the river of my mind

SOMEWHERE ON THE PINE RIVER — I'm paddling my kayak around a bend, and I see my buddy Pete waving to me from up on a bluff. This worries me, because Pete is also supposed to be paddling.

Straight ahead a very large log juts halfway across the river. Just beyond it, rapids laced with big rocks churn. OK, this is why Pete is on the bluff.

"Stay close to the log!" Pete yells. "Then go to your right!"

Suspect advice from a guy who is soaking wet but whatever. Pete has steered me right throughout this two-hour trip, so I try to do what he says.

But once past the log, no way am I veering right. It's all I can do to keep facing forward.

A few racing heartbeats later, I've bobbed safely over the roiling waters.

So went the final challenge of my foray down the Pine River, which runs swift and scenic through the Manistee National Forest. I've seen many a canoeist drink deep of its bracing waters. Thanks to good luck and Pete, I stayed dry this day.

Granted, we're not talking a West Virginia whitewater adventure here. But this river is challenge enough for a guy with minimal boating skills. Even the apparently peaceful Pine can be perilous if you get stuck under the wrong log.

This knowledge tends to keep your mind in the present tense, which is something I'm working on lately.

Thinking in the present is a way to be present, which is a way to know who you are at any given moment. Like all physical and spiritual disciplines, it's no cinch to master. Paddling the Pine is good practice.

I glide for long, stretches on smooth water. I survey the riverbank, rising high to a crown of pretty pines and birches.

I listen to the birds and the rushing water, think about my yard back home, where I'm trying to grow grass, but I'm so darn busy with that story I'm writing ...

Whoa, look out! Big rock ahead, mid-river. "Go left!" Pete calls behind him. I do, barely missing the brute.

My mind snaps back into the present, realizing it can't afford to stray elsewhere for long.

Here, mindfulness is at least enforced by the river. On land, it's even harder to attain.

Meditators are good at it. They sit for long spells focused on their breathing or a mantra. When their monkey-mind starts skittering away, they gently but insistently call it back to the present.

Even then, once you de-lotus you have work to do. And if you're like me, whatever task you tackle or pleasure you indulge is bollixed by your brain's constant wanderings into the past and future.

Some call this brain busyness a source of perpetual suffering. In his spiritual guidebook "The Power of Now," Eckhart Tolle pinpoints incessant, worrying and regretful brain-talk as something that separates us from others and our true being.

"The mind is a superb instrument if used rightly," Eckhart writes, but adds, "you usually don't use it at all. It uses you."

Make now your dwelling place and visit the past and future only when needed to solve problems or make plans, he suggests.

Good advice for a guy like me, who tends to miss the moment by thinking about other times and places.

When you really try to focus on the present, it is amazing how quickly the mind wants to take you somewhere else.

The present, of course, is all we really have, and it can be taken from us with stunning swiftness.

So, do we just live for today? Certainly not. We need to make plans and build futures for ourselves, our kids and communities. But surely we do well to live in today, fully live the gift of the present and not let our busy brains worry it away.

That is why I like rivers. They're lovely, ever-present and you can't see around the bend.

May 28, 2005

Cleaning out clutter, below and above

It began with water. Water gushing into my basement like a fire sprinkler in a hotel hallway, sprung loose by a crack in the water pipe leading outside. No, I did not leave the hose attached all winter! Although maybe a little too long last fall. Doesn't matter.

This is what 90-year-old houses do. Ten colorful words later, my basement carpet was soaked.

It was in pulling up the carpet that I saw them, fallen from their shelves: Hamilton's Guide to Yellowstone. The Mountain Biker's Guide to the Great Lakes. AAA tour books to Europe and every region of America.

And the maps! Wrinkled maps to Florida, New York, Oregon, the weathered documentation of trips past and possibly future. How long had these maps been stored down here, like dusty seafaring charts in a ship's hold? How long since I had gone to any of the places they described? What use could they be?

And yet here they lie, and here I sat, unwilling to pitch them, as if doing so would be throwing away my long-held hopes for high seas adventure.

Then over here, peeking from beneath an old file cabinet, the assembly manual for a Fisher Price trike. This would have been for my son, now 23. This gives you some idea how long it had been since I cleaned the basement, also called The Place Where Everything Else Goes.

Just beyond the cabinet, stacks of old toys mocked my desire to shed the past. Lincoln Logs. Legos. Pickup Sticks. Colorforms! And not a grandchild in sight. Again, what use?

This is where I leave the basement to its dank smell, shelves of Zane Grey books and musty record albums. The shedding of them is too much. Too many decisions to make, too many memories stirred.

It's like this every time I try to simplify my life. I want to let go of the past and end up being swallowed by it. This goes with what I choose to call "maturing."

As the years pass, many of us have the urge to simplify. Lighten the load of possessions, and spiritual serenity will grow. Get it down to a reading chair and a breakfast nook, and enlightenment surely will follow.

I wonder how the Buddha found the willpower to shed his princely garments and lavish lifestyle to become a voluntary beggar. Did he not want to at least take his copy of "Frampton Comes Alive!" on his way to Nirvana?

For all that has been written, spoken and dreamed about cleaning the clutter from our lives, it remains a formidable challenge. In a society where buying things is essential to the economy, goods pile up faster than you can discard them. Life is one big neighborhood yard sale: You end up getting more stuff than you get rid of.

But material clutter is but a dust bunny compared to the emotional debris of the soul. Regrets, resentments, hurts and disappointments quietly accumulate until you're heavy with the effort of hauling them around.

Call me a New Age leftover, but I find clearing useless stuff from the basement helps point the way to healthy soul-cleaning.

In this, I consider throwing away keys a major achievement.

A rack of them had sat on a high shelf for years. I took them down the other day and realized I didn't know what a single one of them opened except for my long-gone Ford Taurus.

Yet a certain fear stayed my hand over the wastebasket. What if one of them opened something that I still own? And what would that thing be? If I throw out the key, it will be locked forever!

Oh well, none of it will matter when the world ends, or my world at least. I pitched nine of them, kept two and felt lighter.

Now on to the toys, books, records and maps, each with its own memories and charms.

Who knew attaining simplicity could be such work?

May 21, 2011

In search of security – or not

These Buddhist sages, they can be so useless.

A Sunday-morning group of us pondered the writings of Ken McLeod, author and teacher of Tibetan Buddhism, on the suffering brought on by desire — especially the desire for security.

"One way we seek to satisfy the desire for security is by having — having a job, a bank account, a house, good looks," McLeod wrote in the magazine "Tricycle." "Yet a violent storm, a car accident, or an upheaval in the financial markets can eliminate in a moment what we regard as 'mine.'"

Uh huh, got it, we nodded. Know just what you mean. And?

"Stop seeking security," McLeod went on. "Time and again I have seen students relax and open to the fullness of life when they understand and accept that there is no security and that they are going to die."

OK, this is really not helping. We pretty much already know we're going to die, and a lack of security is exactly our problem. What else you got, McLeod?

Let's see, it's something about accepting that the things you own aren't really yours, and letting yourself experience desire without acting on it.

See what I mean about useless?

Well, not entirely. McLeod helpfully suggests renouncing a desire for security that isn't attainable. Death, he writes, "shows us that even our life isn't ours."

I detected an echo of Jesus' "whoever loses his life for my sake will find it." Grasping for material security takes you farther from the real thing, many faiths agree. Yachts and 401(k)s need not apply.

But pray tell, Jesus, Buddha and all ye life coaches: What do I do with this rampant sense of insecurity? This thing that wakes me up with a knot in my stomach and questions in my head: Where will the money come from? When will the job materialize? Can I really afford a dishwasher?

Keep in mind these are the anxieties of a man with work, albeit part time. What must it be like to have no job and no prospects — new dishwasher out of the question? With national unemployment above 10 percent, we have cold comfort in knowing we're not alone. In fact, most of the people I know are in this boat, employed or not.

Those blessed with jobs are working harder than ever but making less. They wonder how long the job will last. And they wonder, in their late 40s to mid 50s, whether they ever will stop working this hard.

The life story many of us took for granted — building the career, having the family, retiring in relative comfort — is beginning to look like a fairy tale.

Retirement? How would that work? I picture Dagwood on his death bed, his boss, Mr. Dithers, at his bedside: "You've met your deadline, Bumstead. It's OK to let go now."

So, then, how to find security in a tsunami economy? Are we back to Ecclesiastes? "All is vanity. What does man gain from all his labor at which he toils under the sun?" Not to mention woman, who probably is toiling harder than man.

I'm a columnist, not a life coach. But living with insecurity is pushing me away from the obvious antidotes.

A full-time job? More money? Sure, those would help greatly. But they won't bring security.

More and more, I'm finding the most security in relationships and meaning.

The relationships we nurture over time give us strength to face whatever comes. Sometimes, they bring helpful connections. Always, they bring aid in adversity and comfort in crisis.

Meaning comes from the way we live and how we treat others. It emanates from moral conviction. For many, it comes from faith, and the God who has seen so many through times worse than this.

Yeah, financial security would be great. But friends and faith — those I can't live without.

Nov. 14, 2009

At peace with those gone before

The words on the tombstone were indistinct, eroded by time and weather. I had to trace my fingers over the letters and numbers as if they were Braille.

Robert Grattan, died Sept. 19, 1872. Age 17 — or was it 12? Too young, in any case, as Robert's epitaph made clear:

"Short was my time, severe my pain. To rest in Christ is now my gain. Dry up your tears and weep no more. I am not dead but gone before."

Rest. That was the right word for this place. Surrounded by more than 4,000 souls gone before, I felt sweet rest.

This was the hill crowning Summit Cemetery, the main burial ground for people from my hometown of Williamston. Under towering pines and lordly oaks lay generations of Williamstonians dating back to the little town's beginnings.

On a late Sunday afternoon, I looked around at the graves of old friends, familiar families and the plots where my mother, father and sister one day will join these resting thousands.

A light southern breeze fluttered American flags on the graves of war veterans. A pinwheel whirred over a baby's burial place. Birds twittered, cicadas buzzed, a mourning dove cooed. Far to the south a train whistle blew, as it has since I was a boy here.

How strange that I should feel such contentment in the midst of death.

Cemeteries exert a peculiar pull on the imagination. In Grand Rapids, I have spent hours walking among the Egyptian obelisks, Celtic crosses and Greek-style temples of Oakhill Cemetery. I've taken autumn afternoon runs through Washington Park Memorial Gardens bordering Catholic, Jewish and Lithuanian burial grounds.

It's not just their natural beauty and serenity that make us linger in cemeteries. It's the sense of mystery surrounding the cycle of life.

In the tiny, unmarked stones and angel-ornamented monuments, we find history, continuity and community. We are born, grow up, work hard and sometimes become known far and wide. But we all end up here. From dust to dust, life to death and, for many believers, to life again.

Early Christians rejoiced that the dead were with God. In our skeptical age, the adage "he's in a better place now" sometimes rings false. But walking Summit Cemetery, I feel sure these departed souls are in a good place, resting at last.

It's like a town reunion. Everywhere I see the familiar names I grew up with: Eaton, Jabs, Oesterle, Wygant. Other names are musically old-fashioned: Sophronia, Egbert, Hezekiah. Still other markers are covered with lichen or toppled, their names forever obscured.

I come across people I didn't know were here but knew in life: Nancy Lightfoot, a United Methodist missionary; Helen Kuehn, my elementary principal; Marguerite Volmar, the kindly, erudite woman who rented my wife and me our first apartment.

Here is Babyland filled with the poignant plots of infants. "Precious daughter," Carol Ann Walker, 1988-89, has a tiny blue rocking horse next to her grave.

A little ways off, wind chimes peal lightly in the breeze, the sound of time passing.

I walk over. By the chimes, side by side, are the graves of two of my classmates: Lawrence H. Graham, 1952-1973, and Steven B. Smith, 1952-1970.

Steve died just before we graduated, a friendly Future Farmer of America killed in a tractor accident. Larry died in another accident. I still think of them as I knew them then, forever wearing yearbook smiles, forever facing a bright future.

One day I will join them, perhaps here with so many others I grew up with, on this graceful hill.

The thought causes me no fear, for it is just too peaceful here. Weep no more, the graves sigh. It's time to rest.

Aug. 13, 2005

Eighth Inning

Around the Horn

New year, ancient yearnings

It is the iconic childhood photo of my extended family, taken in my grandparents' Detroit home over the holidays.

I'm guessing it's about 1962, judging from the Sandra Dee flip of my teen sister Maureen's hair. My brother, Mike, and I are wearing ties, which can only mean we were forced into them by church or the formality of the photo session. There are 19 of us cousins, 16 of them emanating from my mother's two brothers. (They were Catholic; we were not.)

We were a big noisy lot. Holidays at Grandma's house meant rampaging through the basement while the grownups played cards. Christmas and New Year's were boisterous, full of children's squeals and the rollicking ragtime Grandma played on her baby grand piano.

Snap the shutter again, and that piano shows up in my parents' living room. Through a trick of the light, the picture has been transformed. My son, Max, is playing Scott Joplin ragtime on Christmas Day. My parents are listening contentedly while my significant other, Andrea, and I clean up the dishes.

My mother's parents have long since crossed the river, as have my father's. Cousins: scattered far and wide, though we keep in touch. The holidays, once as raucous as church bells pealing, are quiet as children sleeping.

I like it that way. Because the world is so much noisier now.

Oh, we had our issues back in 1962. For a moment there, it looked like the Cuban missile crisis might put an end to it all. The University of Mississippi exploded in riots over the enrollment of a black student, James Meredith. Never let nostalgia fool you into thinking things were better then.

But they were assuredly less complicated and noisy. TV's three networks went off at night with a test pattern. My cousins' happy racket drowned out the tube. Music came down on turntable spindles, and transistor radios tinnily transmitted the Beatles' first single.

The 21st century comes at you nonstop. Bombs explode in Kabul and angry pundits blow up on cable news. Cars boom like traveling concert stages, and every other driver is on a cell phone. As the Grinch put it, "Oh, the noise, noise, noise, noise!"

Is this the future, then? Ever noisier, harsher and more complicated? And we ever more aware of the latest foiled plot to blow us up, child kidnapping or unemployment rate?

But perhaps this, too, is a trick of the light.

The surface of life speeds up at louder volume, but its essence remains unchanged. At day's end, we still want a good meal, a sound sleep and a loving family. The spiritual still pray with faith in God or a benevolent universe.

The deepest question still is "Why?" And the deepest prayer still is "Thank you."

You want to give thanks on the first day of a new year, or, in this case, a new decade. Put it on your lips as you take a long walk around the neighborhood. Breathe it in as you look around the dinner table, just after grace. Dream on it as you gaze on the Christmas lights, as did your ancient ancestors who built fires to coax the sun back to the dark mid-winter.

Underneath the noise, we still are those ancient people, wondering why we had the hardships of the past year but thankful for the blessings of a new one. Only now the lights we gaze upon are brilliant LED strands lighting up the neighborhood bright as bonfires.

Such miracles we have now! I imagined the future would bring flying cars. Instead, it brought flight to the palm of my hand. This much-too-smart phone takes me anywhere I want to go. History of Christmas lights? Just touch "Google," and I'm there. Incredible!

Again, though, it's just a trick of the light. Technology has made the world smaller but not warmer over these thousands of years. For warmth, we still go inside: into our memories, our faith, our families and homes.

That's where the brightest lights dwell like a pack of noisy cousins, even on a quiet New Year's Day.

Jan. 1, 2011

A Christian comes home to Judaism

Paula Bojsen has scrubbed her house from top to bottom, and it's not just spring cleaning. She has been emptying her shelves of bread, pasta and any other leavened foods in preparation for Passover, the Jewish holiday that begins tonight at sundown.

Her strict observance of Jewish kosher laws is not something she would have anticipated five years ago, when she was an evangelical Christian.

Although new to Judaism, she finds deep meaning in Passover's celebration of the Hebrews' exodus from Egyptian slavery.

"We have a Jewish soul," said Bojsen, 49, who converted in 2002. "Our souls were present at Sinai as well," when God gave Israelites the Ten Commandments.

"For me, Judaism is the legitimate, God-ordained religion."

She and her husband, Tom, are among a small number of Christian converts to Judaism in West Michigan. It's a lengthy process that involves not only learning the traditions and teachings of Judaism but giving up Christian beliefs — and perhaps Christian friends.

Anywhere from a few to 10 people a year convert at Congregation Ahavas Israel, the Bojsens' Conservative synagogue. Rabbi David Krishef oversees the process, which ends with converts appearing before a Jewish court in Detroit. There, they immerse themselves in a ritual bath and renounce their prior faith — including belief in Jesus as their savior.

That is to ensure people are spiritually ready and do not convert only to promote Jesus as the Jewish messiah, Krishef said.

"I have no motivation to turn sincere Christians into Jews," Krishef said. "I would like to know for sure that they are absolutely committed to living a Jewish life within a Jewish community for the rest of their life."

At Temple Emanuel, a Reform congregation, Rabbi Michael Schadick oversees a few conversions per year. His process is less stringent, ending with a ceremony of blessings and prayers in which he gives converts a Hebrew name.

"Most people are disaffected Christians who either have not found meaning in a Christian denomination or have questioned Christian theology, and Judaism seems to make more sense," Schadick said.

That was the case for Paula Bojsen. Long nagged by doubts about Christianity, she began studying Judaism as part of a Bible study.

"Everything I read touched me more and made more sense than Christianity did," said Paula, who was active in a variety of churches.

She found in Judaism a faith where she could speak directly to God and not be threatened with damnation if she questioned the teachings.

Her husband likes the Torah's emphasis on gradual self-improvement. Both relish the weekly Sabbath, in which they forgo work for 24 hours.

"Your soul is at peace," Paula said. "You don't drive. You don't turn on the TV. It's family time."

Their conversion has not been without cost, although generally people have been accepting.

"You lose some friendships," Paula said. "But the ones who really mattered to me said, 'We can talk about that sometime, but we really care about you.'"

Their daughter, Joanna, 10, who takes Hebrew classes, says her public-school classmates are intrigued by her faith.

"Some kids are interested in a different culture," Joanna said. "There's not many people who criticize me just because I'm Jewish."

As she prepared to attend a Passover Seder, Paula rejoiced in being part of an ancient tradition.

"It feels like we've come home," she said. "It feels like this is where we should be."

April 23, 2005

For faithful servant, believing is seeing

It was the afternoon of Good Friday, just before Christian tradition says Jesus drew his last breath.

But to Lester DeKoster, his savior was every bit as alive as I was, sitting by his bedside.

Such is the faith of a man who may soon draw his last breath. Or not. Either way, Jesus was very much alive for him this day, and not just because he has spent a lifetime following him.

Certainly, Jesus was alive in the loving care of Colleen Murphy, a Faith Hospice nurse aide. Her smile was as welcome as the sunlight glittering off the Thornapple River outside the picture window of the DeKoster home.

"Thanks for coming," Lester said after she gave him a parting hug. He looked after her warmly. "It doesn't hurt to fall ill in Grand Rapids," he confided with a twinkle.

Lester suffered congestive heart failure after Thanksgiving and has been in hospice care since Christmas. The past few weeks, he has not gotten out of his bed in the living room of his Cascade Township home.

There, with his wife, Ruth, he receives visitors and watches songbirds on the deck outside where he and Ruth used to sit.

For a man about to turn 94, it is a season to be expected, even savored. He has four loving children, nine grandchildren and a full life to look back on. As a former Calvin College librarian and editor of the Christian Reformed Church magazine The Banner, he has had an interesting, if sometimes controversial, career.

"It's been a good time," he said softly. "I'd do it over."

For him, Jesus lives in these memories of a life resting firmly on the faith Christ died for his sins, then showed up on Easter to stunned disciples.

Lester needed no further evidence that Jesus lives.

He got it anyway.

"He was here," he told me in a choked-up voice. "He was dressed in a long robe. He said, 'What you've been told is true.'"

He's not real comfortable talking about this. Lester is a thoughtful man, his faith informed by the cerebral sobriety of the Dutch Reformed. He dreads the tabloid-style headline, "I saw Jesus!"

And yet, Lester must admit, he did. One morning, a couple of weeks ago. There, at the foot of his bed.

"We stood together in the garden," Lester said, looking into the distance. "And he spoke encouragingly. He likes what I was doing."

"He told you that you'd been a faithful servant," Ruth said, supportively.

"That's what he did say," Lester affirmed.

The whole encounter was rather ordinary, though extraordinary, he said.

"It's like saying, 'We went hiking last week, my friend and I.' Yes, we did."

He has no doubt it happened, yet rubs his forehead in wonder. "Yes, I did see Jesus. Can that have happened? I guess so.

"Oh, I can picture it so plainly."

His Jesus encounter doesn't add proof to what he already believed. His faith always rested comfortably on the Apostle Paul's assertion, "We fix our eyes not on what is seen, but on what is unseen."

But seeing Jesus certainly was a comfort, he said, and a nice affirmation as he prepares for the next life.

He looks forward to seeing his dear departed friend Duncan Littlefair, the former Fountain Street Church minister with whom he loved debating theology.

"Probably the first one I'll see," Lester said with a quiet chuckle. "We'll compare notes."

Littlefair — who always proclaimed his non-belief in a life hereafter — might scoff when Lester tells him about his visitation from Jesus. So might you.

You might also ask, why is belief in something seen any less credible than faith in the unseen? Who is to judge what another perceives to be true?

I left Lester content with his perception, and grateful for it. He took my hand and said, "Someday, we'll meet on the other side and it will all become clear."

I'll put my faith in that any day.

April 18, 2009

Easter faith defies death's sting

Easter is full of mystery. The Resurrection defies all human logic and experience, but brings believers to their feet with song. "Lives again our glorious king! Where, O death, is now thy sting?" many Christians will sing while joyfully bearing a cross, an instrument of agonizing death. As Philip Yancey once wrote, can you imagine people wearing little electric chairs around their necks?

It is a powerful mystery how people of faith can rise up from whatever beating life has given them — the devastation of divorce, the hell of addiction, the grief of a lost child — and proclaim their faith in the risen Christ and a good God.

The magnificent mystery is the hymn of victory over death, and the faith of those who sing it. How remarkable that Christians sing that song with joy, even after death has dealt them such cruel blows.

How will the people of Grand Rapids' Crossroads Bible Church sing it on Easter Sunday, just four days after the funeral of their youth pastor, Derek Taatjes, and his infant son, Dylan James?

How can they sing joyfully of Christ's defiance of death, whether in a classic hymn or Christian rock praise, barely a week after these two sons of God died in a house fire?

I suspect it has a lot to do with Derek, 34, who loved to run and preach and inspire young people about "blazing for Jesus." At his funeral at Calvary Church, his good friend Steve Van Poolen called Derek "an unstoppable force for God."

For fervent believers like these, God's power doesn't stop at death. Death is not a coffin but a doorway. It leads to life with Jesus, for whom Derek lived so passionately.

"I'm missing my friend," Van Poolen told me. "But I have a firm hope of not only where he's at and what he's experiencing, but that I will have the opportunity to see him again."

Hope. The word pulsates at the heart of the Christian faith. It empowered Lutheran pastor Dietrich Bonhoeffer to resist the Nazis and pay for it with his life; it sustained Mother Teresa as she served wretched Calcutta beggars while struggling with agonizing doubts about God.

It may be upholding Charity Taatjes now, as she struggles to cope with the death of her husband and the father of their daughters, Ella and Johanna.

Crossroads Pastor Rod Van Solkema urged the hundreds at Derek's funeral to hold onto hope even as they mourned, to think of him as being awakened by Jesus.

"I ask you to place these deaths in Jesus, because Derek put his life there," Van Solkema told them.

Mourning and hope; grieving and joy; death and waking up: How do such things hold together?

Most call it faith: "the assurance of things hoped for, the conviction of things not seen," as the Bible tells it. Skeptics sometimes mock this faith as wishful thinking. Over many years of writing about religion, I have been humbled by it time and again.

I have seen this Easter faith in a woman giving prayers and crackers to drunks and prostitutes on South Division Avenue; in a pastor who forgave his brother's murderers and a woman who forgave her rapist; in a priest who was paralyzed, only to rise up and give communion from his wheelchair.

Christians will celebrate Easter on Sunday. It may seem like a mystery. But for Derek Taatjes and his fellow believers, it's as natural as waking up and singing.

April 23, 2011

We gather at the river, sins and all

Something in the way the sunlight reflected off the river, dappling the underside of the old cement bridge with rippling lines, pulled me fully into an exquisite American moment.

On top of the bridge, three older men held flags over the water — two Stars and Stripes and an American Legion banner. Next to them stood a few other older men holding rifles. Two women from the VFW Auxiliary stood by, holding flowers.

Below, lining the shaded banks of the Red Cedar River, scores of families looked up. Parents holding children, teens in jeans, seniors in light jackets squinted at the perfect blue sky and listened to the names of young men who died in wars.

It was Memorial Day morning in Williamston, the small mid-Michigan town where I spent most of my childhood. I don't always get to the annual parade through town and the gathering at the river. This year I did. I was grateful I made it.

God and country. Duty and honor. Sweat and sacrifice. Corny ideas, all. In my generation, many of us have regarded patriotism and flag-waving with a skeptical eye.

Too many Vietnam horrors, too much Watergate jaundice, too keen an awareness of America's sins have dimmed the flag's splendor for us. We were repulsed by those who self-righteously brandished it like a saber and told us to love America or leave it.

Most of us continued to love it, but with some sense of diminishment. We might stand through "The Star-Spangled Banner" at ball games, but we never again would recite the Pledge of Allegiance.

Sometimes, it takes awhile to rediscover the beauty of something you have tossed aside. It takes time and wisdom to realize your own self-righteousness, judgmental nature and lack of understanding. To see, among the sins you rightfully have abhorred, the good things that have helped make your life a blessing.

At our house, we put out the flag on July 4, even though we do not agree with everything America does or has done. We also pray at our church, even though we do not agree with everything the church does or has done. With the same thinking, we pay our taxes, support our schools and contribute to our community.

All that said, it has not been easy to maintain the kind of faith in America that actually touches the heart. Sure, we're a great country, but what does that mean exactly? Our high standard of living? How about the high number of people murdered, divorced or incarcerated? What does patriotism mean in such a problematic society?

Where is the sweet, simple love of country that once moved us to put our hands over our hearts and sing well out of our range?

I tasted just a bit of it by the river on Memorial Day. It tasted sweet indeed, and refreshing.

First, we watched the high school and middle school bands march through the downtown four corners. The rattling drums and blaring trumpets never sounded so good. The Boy Scouts and Girl Scouts trooped by proudly. Dozens of adults and kids toted a flag huge enough to catch a sky diver. The fire engines flashed their lights.

Then, we gathered at the river, as they always do in Williamston on Memorial Day. In front of me, a little girl with a ponytail hung on her mom's shoulder, holding a tiny flag. I didn't know most of the people around me, but we were bound by something deeper — love of this little town, and this country of countless like it.

The local Methodist minister led a brief prayer. Then, veteran Earl Salisbury, as much a Memorial Day fixture as the bridge he stood on, read the names of Williamston men who died in battle.

After each name, a band member made a brief drum roll. One of the guys went to high school with my brother.

Two buglers played taps. Two jet planes roared overhead. The old vets fired their rifles. The VFW ladies tossed garlands into the river. The flowers floated downstream.

It all seemed a pretty modest remembrance for soldiers who knew the nightmares of Normandy and napalm. A glorification of death? No, not today. I saw affirmation of life, a good life for which people have died.

It was a life we quietly celebrated, despite its sins, with songs and prayers. A country could do worse.

June 3, 2000

Muslims hunger to nourish the spirit

Joe Jangda strolled up to the Islamic Center and Mosque of West Michigan shortly after 8 p.m. on the second day of Ramadan.

He had not eaten a thing or sipped a drop of water since 5:30 a.m. But the Sparta man insisted he felt great.

"I feel a lot better than two days ago," said Jangda, 60, and patted his tummy with a grin. "Some of the stuff from last year is coming off."

Though he'd eaten nothing all day but a bowl of cereal and a banana, Jangda looked forward to losing a little weight and gaining spiritual benefits during the Muslim holy month.

Nor did he mind that Ramadan's daily fast this year lasts nearly 15 hours. Because of Islam's lunar calendar, the holy month falls about 11 days earlier each year on the Western Gregorian calendar. It's now trending toward the longer, hotter days of summer.

"You'd be surprised how little you need to survive," said Jangda, minutes before partaking of the fast-breaking meal called iftar at the Burton Street mosque.

"God's saying, 'Think about the person who's hungry for three days, how they feel. You're only hungry for 15 hours.'"

Then he headed inside for the meal and late-night prayers — all part of the Ramadan ritual for West Michigan Muslims.

Besides observing the daylight prohibition against eating, drinking and sex, Muslims increase their charitable giving and gather for nightly recitations of the Quran.

Such fasts are physically demanding but spiritually invigorating, local Muslims say.

"It's not that bad," said Saif Islam as he dug into the iftar meal at the Islamic Center. "But it would not be fasting unless it's a little bit difficult. That's kind of the point."

Next to him, Brook Davis gratefully ate the first food he'd had since downing a hamburger before dawn. While working at the Grand Rapids wastewater treatment plant he had done his best to think not about food, but about his relationship with God.

"When I first became a Muslim, it was so hard," said Davis, who converted about 15 years ago. "I was getting dizzy spells."

Now, he finds the fast helps him "appreciate what you have 24 hours a day," knowing others have far less.

That also holds true for Muslim moms and their football-playing sons.

Debbie Mageed said she was a little concerned about this Ramadan having the longest days since she converted to Islam about 10 years ago. But she has found her body has adjusted despite having blood-sugar problems. Focusing on God's role in that is one of Ramadan's major benefits, she says.

"When you're fasting 15 hours and getting through it without hardly feeling any hunger or thirst, you know that God is helping you through that," said Mageed, of Grand Rapids Township.

This week, she made sure to provide nutritious breakfasts of eggs, bagels and cream cheese to her children, Adam, 14, and Sarah, 11, who are both fasting. The morning meal is especially valuable to Adam, a freshman playing football for Forest Hills Northern High School.

Mageed said she talked to Adam's coach, who assured her Adam should let him know when he needs a break during the three-hour practices. Drinking water would break the fast, but he can rinse out his mouth out and cool himself with a wet washcloth.

Still, Adam overextended himself in practice one day this week, prompting a sit-down with his parents.

"We had to make him understand he can't be pushing his body to the limit like that," she said.

For Ali Metwalli, Ramadan fasts are just mind over matter. A finance professor at Western Michigan University, he taught evening classes this week, pausing at 8:15 for tea and a few dates.

"Ramadan is a mindset," Metwalli said. "If you start the month knowing there is no eating or drinking from this time to this time, it's like putting your disk in the computer. It's the only program that will function."

Back at the Burton Street mosque, Salman Azim enjoyed the iftar meal before reciting his late-evening prayers. After a day of working at Steelcase, the Grand Rapids Township man showed no weariness.

"It's just the spirit of Ramadan; it gives you strength," Azim said. "I am more happy in Ramadan. It's a blessed month."

Sept. 6, 2008

A simple 'thank you' will suffice

Grace so often comes unsought and unearned. Monday night at Fountain Street Church, I walked right into it.

In a high-ceilinged alcove off the sanctuary, five full-throated male singers had set up shop following an interfaith service. Filled with the evening's spiritual generosity, the Westminster Presbyterian Church quintet treated a dozen or so passers-through to their heavenly harmony.

"Holy, holy, holy, Lord God almighty," they sang, their splendid voices reverberating into the upper reaches of the Tower Room.

We listened as if we had happened upon a cluster of angels. Then some of us joined in on a rhapsodic round of "amens," which for a moment seemed to lift the veil between heaven and earth.

It was grace, pure and simple. The only right response was "thank you," delivered in my case with a hearty handshake.

Thank you: Perhaps it's possible to carry that thought as a kind of walking prayer, as we enter this time of grace and wonder.

It's not my first thought each morning, to be honest. That's more likely to be, "Go away, let me sleep" as I burrow deeper into the covers. After all, it's dark, it's cold, and there is too darn much to do out there.

If it weren't for Thanksgiving, many of us would fly apart at the seams about now. We're racing along on the fast track of task-oriented fall, and soon the path will be covered with snow. For those of us who are Christmas-oriented, the way to peaceful Bethlehem seems strewn with a million minor to-do's.

This Thanksgiving weekend offers a place to pause and breathe deeply, even if it does involve minor skirmishes at the mall. If you're looking for a reason to give thanks, here it is.

Bemoan your busy, hard life if you must, but allow yourself the grace of gratitude for all you have and have to give.

You might take a cue from Sister Sue Tracy. The Dominican nun with a buoyant spirit breathed peace into the interfaith crowd at Fountain Street, her serenity spreading through a sanctuary filled with Christians, Jews, Muslims, Buddhists, Quakers and Hindus.

"If the only prayer you say in your entire life is 'thank you,' that will suffice," Tracy said, quoting the Christian mystic Meister Eckhart.

Calling Thanksgiving "gratitude in action," the Spectrum Health chaplain broke down the word's letters into a series of blessings: talents, humor, abundance and so forth.

A four-time cancer survivor, she even gave thanks for illness as a way to learn how precious life is, be more compassionate to others and be grateful for their help in healing.

When she came to the letter "n," she transfixed us with a meditation on the blessing of now.

"I thank God for now, for this moment, in this place," she said in her quietly radiant voice. "Life isn't one day at a time. Life is one breath, one blink, one swallow, one heartbeat at a time."

You could almost hear the heartbeats. There we all were, Christians in clerical collars, Jews in yarmulkes, Sikhs in turbans, sharing this moment in this place, all thankful in our way for the gift of being.

"There is one God with many names; we are all the children of God," chanted four Sikh girls in brilliantly colored clothes.

"O God beautiful, at thy feet O I do bow," sang Fred Stella in a Hindu chant.

"Don't forget where all your blessings come from," sang a gospel quintet, their fervor prompting the quiet crowd to clap along.

Just being present was a blessing not to be forgotten. In a world ripped by religious hatred, we shared our many faiths without judgment and left with one prayer on our lips: thank you.

For now, that will suffice.

Nov. 25, 2006

Wonder works its Christmas magic

Christopher deVinck can still see the long, veined hands of his father holding a toy soldier and turning the key.

It was a moment of unexpected intimacy. Jose deVinck had taken an instant to show young Christopher how to work the soldier, just out of its Christmas package.

Why this image should stick with Christopher, now a 44-year-old author, is curious. Surely more dramatic things have happened in his life. But this moment held something rare and lasting.

Wonder.

The resonance of the word itself suggests its rarity. You can't apply it to too many things. When you experience wonder, you feel it. When you don't, you feel that, too.

Amazement, suspense, adrenaline highs: Those you can get at a movie theater, a football game or a Cedar Point ride. Wonder is not obtainable. You just have to notice it when it happens.

Personally, I don't notice it often enough.

DeVinck made a point of noticing by writing about it in his new book, "Simple Wonders," published by Zondervan of Grand Rapids. A hand-sized collection of meditations, the book describes such wonders as ordinary trees, elephants or an old woman who says she has God in her knitting basket.

It begins with deVinck skating on a frozen swamp as a boy. He stopped, kneeled and swirled his glove on the ice's surface. Through the glassy ice, he saw a goldfish looking up at him.

"Under the surface of our lives, there are things swirling around that if we don't clear the ice, we're not going to see it," deVinck told me during a visit to Grand Rapids. A school language arts supervisor from New Jersey, deVinck publishes thought pieces for The Wall Street Journal and other periodicals.

I listened fairly patiently. I had to decide to focus on the conversation, feeling the pressure of things to do pushing on my mental periphery. Even now, other tasks tug at my attention as I write. News events demand to be covered, issues beg to be addressed, our house must be made ready for the season.

So to sit and write about something as ephemeral as wonder seems an indulgence. What does wonder really have to do with people's lives?

Perhaps not a tremendous amount. But I have to question if we need it more than we think.

"Marvel, miracle, (archaic) magical," says my dictionary. "A cause of astonishment or surprise." "Star of wonder, star of might," goes the old carol. "Thou art the God that doest wonders," reads Psalm 77. Of Isaiah's several names for Christ, the first is wonderful.

The wonder of the shepherds in the Christmas story is palpable, and all who heard their story wondered at it. There is fear, awe and delight wrapped up in the Nativity story. Debates over its historical details are merely interesting; what moves us is the wonder.

Perhaps that's why deVinck finds a readership in the no-nonsense Wall Street Journal for stories such as going fishing with his son. A ladybug frozen in the moonlight merits three pages in "Simple Wonders."

He learned his sense of wonder from his mother, Catherine, who would point out a glowing moon or a rustling leaf. He's not sure why wonder is important.

"I just know focusing on those tiny things makes the sad things and the lonely things less sad and less lonely," he says. "Focusing on the simple things teaches us a real sense of gratitude."

He finds gratitude in the memory of his father's caring hands. I find it, among other places, in our Christmas tree.

Outside, it was an ungainly green tangle held upright in a biting wind by a brave tree-seller. Inside, it spreads majestically and glows with a hundred dangling memories. After a day of deadlines, hassles and shoving shoppers, I gaze at our tree and find stillness and wonder.

Like deVinck, I'm not sure why it's important to gaze at a gussied-up tree. But I know without wonder, the days feel mechanical, incomplete and sometimes downright nasty.

Particularly at this time of year, something more wants to be seen and felt. A brief glimpse of the ongoing miracle of creation; a tiny twinge of awe, fear and delight, gently feeding one's sense of gratitude that there really is something to celebrate here.

Too often we look right past those wondrous moments, and the goldfish under the ice slips away.

Dec. 16, 1995

Angels we have heard nearby

A remarkable man passed away three weeks ago, though you probably didn't mark his passing.

His name was Fred Ritsema. Mr. Ritsema was not a news-maker. But he once told me a Christmas story that was, of the many I have heard over the years, the most remarkable.

He returned home from World War II on a Friday. The following Monday, he stuck out his thumb on Chicago Drive SW to hitchhike to Australia, where he'd met Edna May Shute at a dance.

Nearly three months of trains, trucks and steamers later, he showed up at her doorstep on Christmas Eve 1945. They married and came back to Grand Rapids, where they lived a good, non-news-making life.

"Jesus, Heavenly Father, bring us together in heaven once more, unending," read his final prayer in his obituary.

Now that's what I call true love, the kind that inspires songs crooned over an old radio while Mom and Dad dance around the living room. Ardent, devoted, sacrificial love. A Christmas kind of love.

Different story, different man, same kind of love: Christmas Eve, early 1950s. My folks have just made the two-hour drive from Toledo to my grandparents' house in Detroit. Hugs and kisses, kids wide-eyed, taking in the old-fashioned tree and dishes of candy. Secretly, my folks unpack our gifts.

Uh-oh, no BB gun. My brother Mike's biggest present, missing in action. I don't know if it was a Red Ryder, but it definitely could put your eye out. That Christmas, Mike wanted it more than anything in the world.

So, after we kids are tucked in, Dad gets in the car, drives back to Toledo, gets the gun, drives back to Detroit. Early

Christmas morning, Mike gleefully opens his gift. Dad manages a bleary-eyed smile.

Insert here your favorite family story of Christmas craziness. Crazy distances traversed, church pageants gone awry, 2 a.m. runs to Meijer for batteries. All because families love each other, and because Christians love this certain baby who showed up in a box of straw.

The latter event had been preceded by a long trek to Bethlehem, a pretty crazy hike for a pregnant teenager. But Mary had been assured by an angel, so Scripture says: Fear not, God favors you, and nothing's impossible with God. OK then, says Mary. Whatever you say, angel.

Her ready acceptance of this rather spooky news set the pattern for all crazy Christmases to come.

The unexpected happens, things change, the world turns upside down. And the angels say, fear not.

Christmas changed in a big way for my family this year, back in July. That's when my mother, a rather boisterous angel in her own right, left this life. But that was just the beginning.

Seven weeks later, Dad's legs went out from under him. Spinal stenosis had finally caught up, choking off his walking nerves. Still deep in grief and in no particular mood to battle, he went under the knife.

This is when God and his angels really went to work — just as they had in Mom's heart surgery 10 years before — through the skilled hands and caring hearts of physicians and caregivers.

The surgery went off without a hitch, the doc coolly clearing backbone from nerve while we kids sweated bullets. Then followed three weeks of rehab at Mary Free Bed Rehabilitation Hospital, where small miracles were performed on Dad's 89-year-old body, and six weeks at Clark on Keller Lake, a United Methodist assisted-living facility where the caring staff and autumn leaves healed his spirit.

The angels throughout this stretch were way too many to fit on the head of a pin or in a newspaper column.

At Mary Free Bed, therapists cheerfully pushed him onto his feet with help from a really cool walker, doctors expertly guided his recovery, nurses shamelessly babied him, a psychologist listened to his broken heart and social workers held his hand every painful step of the way. One particular social worker close to my heart brought him yogurt and his morning paper.

At Clark, caring nurses and aides attended to his every need, cooks prepared delicious meals, friendly residents chatted with him about their respective journeys into walkers and wheelchairs. Meanwhile, back home, neighbors watched the house and watered the plants to prepare for his return.

Dad came home in early November, driven by my brother who wouldn't touch a BB gun now if you paid him. He stayed with Dad for a month, I stayed for a week, and now my sister is home for several months. Mom's special chair is empty, but her spirit still dances through the house.

Dad has accepted her passing bravely though sorrowfully. Nothing can ever be the same, and this sure isn't the Christmas we expected. But it is Christmas nevertheless, and we will celebrate it in a new way.

And all these angels in the wings whisper, "Fear not."

Dec. 24, 2011

Ninth Inning

Safe at Home

My Mom, the miracle

The little wooden Madonna was the first miracle. She appeared out of thin air at my mother's hospital bedside. Or so Mom thought. All she knew was that suddenly one day, there was the 2-inch Madonna — the same one she had given to my Uncle Chuckie more than 40 years ago.

What she didn't know was Chuckie had slipped into her room while she was sleeping and left Mother Mary there. He had driven all the way from his Port Huron-area home to leave the tiny statue.

He figured it had worked for him when he underwent neck surgery those many years ago. It was time for Mary to keep Mom company, now that she faced open-heart surgery.

In the days that followed, I saw other miracles at work in Mom's life. They were the miracles that arise from skilled hands, space-age technology and compassionate care.

These things came at a time when many of us celebrate miracles. It may be the miracle of a divine baby's birth in a simple stable, with scary angels saying strange things to random shepherds. Or it may be the miracle of a one-day supply of oil burning for eight days in an ancient Jewish temple.

People interpret these miracle stories in various ways from literal to figurative. Some say maybe it happened, maybe not, but they love the idea.

These past two weeks, I've seen things that make miracles as real as my next breath. Anyone who has seen God's grace in a surgeon's hands, or heard the rustle of angels' wings in a nurse's cheerful voice, knows just what I mean.

My wife and I had seen this before at the birth of our daughter. From the first dark days of her premature entry into the world, Emily's life was saved by the dedicated doctors and amazing machines at Lansing's Sparrow Hospital.

Twenty-one years later to the month, we were back there again at Mom's bedside. Worsening episodes of heart failure had put her there. Finally, a probe pinpointed the culprit: a badly leaking valve. The good news was they could fix it — with open-heart surgery.

Anyone who has been close to it knows how not good that news feels. My brother and sister flew in, and we all fretted long days away with my dad. I knew the chances of success were great, but I didn't want any chances at all. I wanted Mom well for sure.

Our fears were eased by Mom's surgeon, Dr. Divyakant Gandhi. As soon as I heard his name, I knew Mom was in good hands. She liked his gentle, confident manner and his Eastern spiritual aura. Using a model heart, he showed us exactly what he was going to do. The night before her surgery, he called her to see if she had any more questions.

Doctors routinely get beat up for being cold, clinical and greedy. Sometimes, it's deserved. But at Lansing Sparrow, I saw the pastoral side of medical care.

Not only did Dr. Gandhi meet with us before and after surgery; Mom's former family practitioner, Dr. David Grimshaw, did also, on his own time. And he spent the better part of a day at Mom's side, in the operating room, watching and praying.

Meanwhile, smiling nurses fluttered their angels' wings, and friends and relatives gathered around Mom like cherubim. She is more spiritual than religious, but she cherished their prayers and gazed gratefully on mini-Mary.

The night before surgery, as she chatted cheerfully, her calm courage floored me. She ate a piece of lemon meringue pie a friend had made her, her spirit centered and her mind ready. This fearless woman was my feisty mom? A miracle.

The next morning, Dr. Gandhi fixed Mom's leaky valve with the finesse of an artist. Aides spooned a salty ice slush around her heart to keep it from beating while a machine pumped her blood and breathed for her. To them, it was routine; to me, it was the stuff of Star Trek.

A nurse came out every hour or so to update us. As we approached five hours we quietly were going frantic. Finally the phone call came: Mrs. Honey is in recovery. Everything went well.

In my heart, I thanked the doctors, I thanked the nurses, I thanked the heart-lung machine and I thanked God, all in approximately two seconds.

As I join millions celebrating miracles of long ago, I am also celebrating the miracles of now: a little statue, a brave mother and the hands of God, donning surgeon's gloves.

Dec. 15, 2001

With change comes pain – and gain

One fall night in 1965, I played football in the back yard until after dark, a spotlight illuminating my attempts to emulate Terry Barr and other Detroit Lions heroes.

Several hours later, I awoke in a panic, unable to move my right leg because of the searing pain. At age 13, I had acquired an old man's injury — a ruptured disc in my lower back.

I will never forget the kind, sad look on my back doctor's face months later, when he told me I would never play football or basketball again. So much for my dreams of becoming the next Richie Jordan, the five-foot-seven Fennville High superstar who could dunk a basketball and tear off 60-yard end runs.

It turned out to be one of the best things that ever happened to me. Instead of warming the bench for four years, as I surely would have, I wrote up the exploits of our high school sports teams for the hometown newspaper. Fate (call him God if you like) had intervened to point me toward my true gifts, not those I only imagined I possessed.

That weak disc has haunted me since, flaring up at odd intervals to jangle the sciatic nerve and remind me of who I am. It hurt like the dickens on my 50th birthday.

Wait a minute — 50? There must be some mistake. Someone spilled the file drawer and mixed me up with my father. I am actually 17, and just on the verge of making major life decisions. Let's see, house painter or rock star?

But no, I really turned 50 this week, weak disc and all. I limped around like Jacob, who wrestled with an angel and got a sore hip for his efforts. He also got a changed name. My sore hip reminded me that change is a good and necessary theme of my life, and usually comes with considerable pain.

I thought a lot about change as I reached what feels like the halfway mark. (For all I know, it may be the nine-tenths mark, but no sense fussing about that.) Whatever and however long the path continues, it probably won't go in the directions I expect.

This goes against the myth of my life journey, in which I was supposed to reach some plateau of maturity and more or less cruise from there.

Of course, some things don't change. On the day I was born, Bob Feller beat the Detroit Tigers, who were beginning one of their worst years ever – just like they are as I write this.

But if I look back at the past half century, change is the main constant in my life and in the world.

My folks got me one of those birthday booklets about "your special year." It tells me that in 1952, England crowned Queen Elizabeth, America tested its first H-bomb, and Pan Am bought the first jet passenger plane. New houses cost $9,000.

The ads brim with post-war, space-age giddiness. Cars are "spectacular," outboard motors "sensational" and the new Admiral TV features an "amazing glare-trap" screen. Another model features a "mammoth" 20-inch tube.

One of my birthday gifts is a color television I can hold in my hand. George Jetson would be thrilled.

The changes in my life have not been spectacular or amazing, but they are remarkable to me.

For one thing, I am a parent, which means I have to make actual decisions and stick by them. I continue to find this very difficult.

I also belong to a traditional Protestant church, an idea that would have gotten me laughed off the family dinner table 40 years ago. Back then, I was singing "Tell Me Why" in Unitarian Sunday School. Then I became a lapsed Unitarian, which is just this side of an existentialist.

But through a process of spiritual discernment – namely, by marrying a United Methodist — I have discovered the blessings of a faith community. Good thing, too. Because in the midst of raising kids, writing stories and rooting for the Tigers, I have had to wrestle with God on several occasions. God always wins. But I always grow.

I also have seen the world become more complicated, problematic and dangerous. Better or worse than 50 years ago, I couldn't say. But it is changing fast. I am, too, more slowly.

It's taken me this long to welcome change, because of all the good things it has brought me: meaningful work, strong faith, dear friends and a beautiful family. The next time my back goes out, maybe I'll accept the consequences more graciously.

June 1, 2002

The Zen of window maintenance

I was cleaning the windows when, thanks to Bill Murray, I re-alized I was living the same day over and over.

Window-cleaning is one of my favorite annual rituals. I do it when the sun is bright, the air is cool and the leaves not yet on the ground. As I wipe away the dusty grime of summer, I think about the gentle passing of time and the blessedness of home. It is part of battening down the hatches, shoring up against winter and stoking the family hearth.

As I wiped away grime, I half-watched a video of "Groundhog Day," that minor classic of comedic theology. Bill Murray por-trays Phil Connors, a jaded Pittsburgh weatherman who gets cosmically trapped in Punxsutawney, Pa., while covering the annual ritual of Groundhog Day.

Connors is appalled to find himself waking up over and over on the same day, condemned to relive it by some sadistic higher power. He careens between reckless self-indulgence and useless suicide, before finding an inner peace in love that liberates him from the wretched cycle of sameness.

As I watched and cleaned, my mind wandered to the fact that I was reliving the same day right then. I have countless times cleaned these windows, on this fall day, feeling these same feel-ings.

Not stopping there, as my mind usually doesn't, I wondered if, like Phil Connors, I was repeatedly not learning what I need-ed to learn to escape the cycle of sameness. I wasn't getting any closer to the deeper purpose of my life. I was just cleaning win-dows, over and over.

Would I be feeling this same way, asking these same ques-tions, at age 85? Still wondering who I am and why I am here, while still wiping away the grime?

It's rather embarrassing to admit to these kinds of questions. I realize many readers, being of a religious or spiritual bent, have moved on to more productive areas. It's sort of like having completed college yet being stuck in first grade in the spiritual development unit.

"I'm so sorry, Johnny, you failed your meaning-of-life test again. But I'm giving you a gold star for effort!"

Maybe I would do better if I studied harder. But who has the time anymore? Between family, work, school, church and "Frasier," I barely have time to read my own newspaper. Oh wait, I didn't do that yesterday either.

And the sad fact is many days do seem to be the same one. Like Phil Connors, I awake each morning at the same time to the clock radio (though unlike him, I do not hear Sonny and Cher each time). I fall asleep 17 hours later at pretty much the same time. In between, life is creative and rewarding but doesn't allow much room to ask what it's all for.

People of certain spiritual persuasions say it's all for learning a lesson. If we don't learn it in this life, we will come back around for another shot.

Others say it's all about forging a relationship with and making a commitment to God. Once there, your life is good on Groundhog Day or any other.

Either way, where I get stuck (back in first grade) is the me-ness of the questions I ask. The me-ness of the one-in-six-billion, one-afternoon-in-eternity nature of a guy cleaning windows, wondering what his life is all about.

And this is important why?

At a certain point, it is almost an insult to life to keep asking. Here I am blessed with another day — clock radio still going off, sun still shining, leaves rattling in the wind — and I have the impertinence to ask what it's for?

But neither does it do to just go through the motions, scarfing down pancakes like the jaded weatherman. Phil Connors finally realized that for whatever reason he was reliving this day, he should make the most of it. He fell in love and gave himself to life — and then which day it was didn't matter.

Deeper sources than Hollywood teach about finding your life by losing it. I don't quite understand how that works. But I sense its truth when I just let the nagging questions sit there and try to give myself completely to this day.

OK, so it's a lot like yesterday. But what was so bad about that?

Oct. 19, 2002

The Good Life was here all along

Advent, circa 1993: The Honey family is wandering through the Amway Grand Plaza Hotel, admiring its gingerbread houses. The hotel's historic halls are sumptuous with Christmas decorations, as we gaze at graham-cracker palaces and candy-cane castles.

Suddenly, my 6-year-old son runs down the hall and shouts gleefully over his shoulder, "Isn't this the *life*?"

I love how kids get overcome with these feelings and just blurt them out. Yes indeed, son, I thought: This is the life. It would never have occurred to me to say it, though.

When I was his age, I thought I wanted nothing more than to grow up. I wanted to be big. Then no one could tell me what to do. I could go to bed when I wanted. I could eat what I wanted. And I could watch whatever I wanted on TV.

Having been big for many years now, I wonder what the rush was. I wish someone would tell me what to do so I wouldn't have to make so many decisions. I really can't eat what I want because it will make me look like Marlon Brando. And I usually am too tired to watch TV.

Being big is not quite the walk down gingerbread lane children think it will be. It is more complicated, confusing and problematic than they can imagine. May they enjoy their candy-cane delights as long as possible.

Still, there comes a time when big people have to stop and smell the gingerbread. Lately, little things tug at my sleeve to say, "Hey, buddy, this really is the life you wanted. Care to enjoy it a little?"

Something about driving along city streets brings these thoughts to mind. Golden leaves rain off trees and pile up on curbs, making me wonder what more I could possibly want.

The colors of dying autumn paint the big picture, and the picture is titled The Good Life.

Tony Bennett sang about it. Children grow up hearing about it. Adults search for it, then forget it's there. Or they may ask, did it ever really exist?

I don't search out The Good Life in the news. I barely can tolerate the daily dose of All Terror All the Time, not to mention the latest child abduction, weird murder trial etc.

Still, this is small potatoes compared to the daily trials of earlier generations who lived through the Dust Bowl, the Depression and world wars. They sucked it up and did what they had to, but they, too, dreamed of The Good Life.

I am of a generation smack in the middle of everything. My friends have parents in the hospital, living with them or already gone. Their children are handfuls. Their jobs keep them up at night. Life is pumping on all cylinders, and the head gasket threatens to blow.

In short, it is a struggle. In the best of times, it still is a struggle to raise children, do your job well and take care of everyone the way you should — while knowing you mostly are falling short. My usual prayer at church is, "Dear God, thanks for letting me fool everyone for another week."

A doctor once said to me, "It's good to be in the struggle and know you're in the struggle." I guess. I want the struggle to go away, but it's what life is made of, pretty much. Again, I didn't know this when I wanted so much to be big.

Back then, I had the idea that I would reach a time in life when I would just coast. I would have everything I wanted and could, more or less, sit back and enjoy it. Actually, I have entertained this fantasy most of my adult life. There would be a time called The Good Life, and I would know it by its easiness.

What a silly idea. Touch down at any point in life and the struggle is there: cramming for exams, heating formula, putting in overtime, meeting with the principal, sitting at the bedside, pushing the walker, murmuring the last prayer.

You are always on the journey, and you never get "there." If The Good Life exists, it is here now, amid the struggle. It's the sun glancing off yellowed leaves, the hot water of a shower, the kid doing his homework.

Is The Good Life real or just a notion we make up to comfort ourselves? I'll choose real. I'd hate to give up on it, then have one of my kids say, "Wow, Dad, didn't you see it?"

Nov. 16, 2002

Fathers and sons, leaving and returning

Back when I was a janitor working my way through college, I was mopping late into the night at the East Lansing Police station when I heard a roar from the TV. I looked up and saw Bernie Carbo trotting the bases. The Boston Red Sox pinch-hitter had hit a three-run homer in the bottom of the eighth, tying it up with the Cincinnati Reds in the sixth game of the World Series.

The cops and I watched amazed. Man, this was some game.

Sure was. Four innings later, Carlton Fisk won it with a dramatic home run and entered baseball lore.

That heart-pounding series in 1975 brought thousands of fans back to baseball, including me. I was 23, and had more or less left the game of my boyhood. By age 17, other interests had taken me far beyond left field.

When the '75 Series brought me back, it also brought me closer to my dad. I had kind of grown away from him, too, for awhile. In my need to become my own man, I distanced myself from Dad, although I never stopped loving him. Our love of the game helped knit us back together.

This going away and coming back of sons is an old theme. It's the rare father who can't identify with Jesus' story of the prodigal son, and the father who runs to embrace and kiss him upon his return. The kid could be coming back from a war, a busted marriage or a drug bust. But he had to go out and prove himself — and probably screw up — before he could come back and submit to that hug.

Mythologist Joseph Campbell calls this the hero's journey. It's the young man's need to go away and have an adventure before he can finally come back home.

I don't claim to know what young women need to do in this regard. I only know what it was like for me and my dad — and what it will be like, most likely, for me and my son.

Today, Max turns 17. I hope he knows how proud I am of him, but it is hard to share that sort of thing with a young man. You might embarrass him.

But I am terribly proud of Max, a gifted, funny, good-hearted young man. I treasure these times with him because it won't be long before he won't be here. He will need to go away.

I know that most of what I can teach Max already has been taught. He does not often come to me for advice, and doesn't often like to hear it when I give it to him.

Baseball is something we, too, have shared. I taught him how to pitch and coached him in youth leagues. But a couple years ago, Max left the game because other interests called to him.

So, the afternoons of playing catch are done. They have been replaced by periodic jam sessions with Max on drums and me on guitar. This is our new way of playing catch, and a blessed connection through the music we love.

Still, I sense the going-away is under way. I wait for moments where I still can have an influence and maybe teach Max one more thing before he stops listening.

The other day I was longing for such an opportunity, almost prayerfully. Later that night it came, as I was watching the Red Sox and Yankees battle it out in their history-making playoff.

Guitar in hand, Max excitedly came down the stairs to show me a song he was working on. He wanted advice on how to fill in the gaps between the verse and chorus.

We worked on it for a half hour, glancing at the game between chord changes. It was a great game of catch, and a gift from God.

The next night, Max and I watched together as, at the stroke of midnight, the Red Sox did what no baseball team had ever done — come back from three games down to win a playoff.

It's a moment I always will cherish. I think Max will, too, one day.

Today, the World Series begins. It figures to be one of the all-time greats, perhaps bringing thousands back to the game as the '75 Fall Classic did.

Dad and I will share the drama. I'm sure Max will watch portions with me, but baseball isn't really his thing right now. Maybe someday he will return to it.

Whether he comes back to baseball or not, what I really care about is he comes back to me.

But I know first I need to let him go away, as young men do. Maybe when he returns, he will want a hug.

It's a mysterious thing. But, oh man, it is some game.

Oct. 23, 2004

Surviving life's battle with bonds of love

My father recently shared with me, in greater detail than he ever has before, how he out-swam death in World War II.

The torpedo plane in which Dad was a belly gunner and radio man ran out of gas on its approach to an aircraft carrier. Within seconds he and his crew mates were bobbing in the huge waves of the South Pacific, trying to swim away from the sinking plane before its depth charges went off.

He remembers the tremendous force of the blast and the flaming debris falling around him. He remembers being pulled onto a ship and, later, his back feeling like someone had pummeled it with a baseball bat.

And he remembers an officer telling him that his good friend, Tom Wolf, hadn't made it. He got out on the far side of the plane and was not a good swimmer.

This experience of death as a young man always stuck with Dad, and, therefore, with me. It is a cautionary tale about how slender life's thread is, how much can depend on so little a difference.

Dad is 83 now. His body is strong and his mind wise with experience. The terrors of his Navy days are long gone.

Yet for him and others of his generation, death is a common occurrence.

It's almost like he's back in combat.

Friends and family fall away left and right. Increasingly, a phone call from Florida is like an officer showing up at the door. With each funeral, life is a little lonelier than it was before.

It is the price of a long and vigorous life: The longer you live, the fewer loved ones are left.

In the combat of life, survival is surely a blessing. But just as surely, it means loss.

Our family experienced a big loss last week.

Uncle Russ seemed like one of those who would be around forever. He had a gentle personality and a warm heart. His 10 children run through the memories of my childhood.

Uncle Russ was my father's high school friend and football teammate. He was my mother's twin brother and soul mate.

Although he was hobbled by hip problems for years, the end came swiftly for Uncle Russ. Complications from surgery led to a heart attack from which he never recovered.

He knew his time had come. He told his children he had lived a rich life and was in the Lord's waiting room.

At his hospital bedside, my mom and dad, Russ' wife, Millie, and I gathered round and said the Lord's Prayer.

At St. Mary Catholic Church in Milford, we gathered in the lobby by his open casket. Cousins poured in and hugged us. Tears and smiles co-mingled. In each other's faces, we saw the years that had passed and the memories that bond us.

In the funeral, the priest spoke of how Uncle Russ lived out God's love. He recalled a Nativity scene Russ built with loving care. Waving incense, the priest said we would still smell it an hour later, just as we would still sense Russ' presence.

At the grave site, Russ' six sons lined up behind his casket, strong and sturdy city men. Huddled with my relatives against the cold, I felt the blood strength of our family. We placed roses on the casket.

Mom still can't believe he's gone. She thinks of him being in the cold, cold ground. I tell her to think, instead, of his warm, living spirit.

This Thanksgiving weekend, we Honey children are gathered around Mom and Dad. The sense of loss is palpable. Yet, so is the sense of years shared in love.

Russ lives in that love we share. His good life has become part of ours. His presence is rich as fragrant incense.

Still standing on the battlefield of life, what do we have to be thankful for? There are not enough words to say.

Nov. 26, 2005

A girl needs someone to dance with

My favorite picture of my daughter, Emily, features her in full Beverly Sills mode.

She is standing by her Fisher-Price record player and happily singing along to a song from Walt Disney's "Cinderella," the book she holds in her hands like a Verdi score. Her head is held high, her chin tilted theatrically upward. She looks like she is singing an aria to thousands at Carnegie Hall, not in our living room singing to me.

That was Emily for you. Ask her to sing a song and she gladly complied, transporting herself to the stage in the process. While other girls her age were rocking to Madonna, Emily dreamed of being Shirley Jones.

Whether watching "Rainbow Brite" on TV, bouncing on the couch to the tune of "Girls Just Wanna Have Fun" or immersing herself in a Berenstain Bears book, Emily sang and danced and read with a joy that seemed to come from someplace bright and beautiful.

My mom always said Emily dropped from heaven. Emily's mother, Wendy, and I felt she had wisdom beyond her years, as if she came into the world already knowing things.

But what Emily did not have, despite dear friends, was one particular friend, one person who cared more about her than about anyone else in the world. That was a person I very much wanted her to meet, because I did not want Emily to go through this hard world alone.

Finally, she met that person. Her name is Nicole.

Emily and Nicki, as I call her, were married three years ago in Massachusetts. At the time, that was the only state where two women, or two men, could get married.

That changed this week, when hundreds of gay couples tied the knot in California after a court ruling that the state's ban on gay marriage violated the state constitution. The judges' 4-3 vote drew on a ruling 60 years earlier that struck down a ban on interracial marriage.

Unlike in Massachusetts, the California ruling allows gay couples from other states to marry there. That's particularly good news for gays in New York, where Gov. David Paterson recently declared state agencies must recognize gay marriages legally performed elsewhere, even though they aren't legal in New York.

Gay marriage opponents are alarmed and swinging into action. Concerned Women for America, a public policy organization, called the California ruling "an affront to God and His plan for marriage and family." A November ballot issue would constitutionally recognize marriage only between a man and a woman.

This is where we are supposed to start arguing about the morality of gay marriage, what the Bible says about homosexuality and whether Ellen DeGeneres is the secret mastermind of the so-called "gay agenda."

Sorry, I can't go there. Yes, there are necessary debates to be had about civil rights, scriptural interpretation and biological realities. But I'm not going to tell you what you should think. That's your job.

All I can tell you is that when this issue becomes personal, everything is different.

It's the difference between saying playground equipment should be safe, and the alarm I felt when Emily got whacked in the mouth by an iron-horse swing. (She sang in the spring concert that night with a missing front tooth.)

When you're the parent of a gay child, the difference is between deciding how you feel about this in your head, and knowing what you feel in your heart. What I feel in my heart is not a passage from Leviticus but the joy of a twirling little girl in a ballerina outfit, longing for someone to dance with.

I don't discount the importance of the theological issues, although if you dive into that pool you'd better be ready to do your homework. "Because the Bible says so" just doesn't cut it when many biblical scholars say the whole of Scripture says something quite different.

And if you care about this issue but aren't personally involved with it, I'd suggest this: Imagine it's personal.

Many say homosexuality is not a sin but homosexual behavior is, therefore gays should either change if possible (which it rarely is) or stay celibate. If that is your answer, please ask yourself, "Would I be willing to do that? Spend my entire life without a loving, intimate relationship with another person?"

I know what my answer is, and I certainly know what I want for Emily. I want her to love and be loved, in a committed relationship. I don't want her to be lonely. Life is hard enough as it is.

Emily and Nicki's life will be harder because many will never accept them, nor do they have the federal tax and legal benefits available to other married couples.

And, by the way, there are hard issues for me, too, things that never will be the way I once dreamed they would be.

But this isn't about my dreams. It's about Emily's, and the wonderful woman who loves her.

They had a delayed wedding party, filled with friends and family both gay and straight. In the middle of it all, Emily beamed with joy.

She could have been singing Cinderella.

June 21, 2008

I sing the goodness of Betty Jean Honey

Music. Betty Jean always loved it, no matter what kind. She grew up in Detroit with my grandpa singing opera and grandma playing ragtime. Betty played piano most of her life, for family Christmas carols, children's church choirs, New Year's Eve parties, banging out "Won't You Come Home, Bill Bailey?" like nobody's business.

Years later, she'd clap for her grandson when he played Scott Joplin on her baby grand. She beamed when her granddaughter sang living-room arias. She'd close her eyes for great music, transported by Pavarotti or Rosemary Clooney or Audra McDonald to someplace very near heaven.

Melody flowed through her veins. That, and politics, and family, and the faces of little children.

"The Lord is my shepherd; I shall not want. He maketh me to lie down in green pastures: he leadeth me beside the still waters."

My mother wasn't much for organized religion. She had no use for its creeds and dogmas and the men who ran the show. She liked my church but was annoyed we talked about God so much. If Mom knew I was quoting the 23rd Psalm, she'd tell me to insert "she" for the God pronouns.

But give her Placido Domingo singing "Ave Maria" and she was the most devout woman ever, her heart filled with divine joy.

"God works through our hands," she said, after a surgeon saved her heart 10 years ago. On that much, we agreed.

"He restoreth my soul: he leadeth me in the paths of righteousness for his name's sake."

Mom's soul thirsted for righteousness. Equal rights and equal care for all people. Protect the poor and the disenfranchised. Be God's hands on earth.

She taught Character School at Fountain Street Church, served on the PTA at Ottawa Hills Elementary. Taught her three kids to respect all people, no matter their color or nationality. Wouldn't even let me watch the Three Stooges because they hurt each other.

Above all, she hated war. Put signs in the yard against it. Wrote letters to the editor. Called up congressmen. Licked envelopes. Stayed on the floor at Democratic Party conventions until everyone else had gone home.

Justice was her religion, to which she was faithful to the end.

"Yea, though I walk through the valley of the shadow of death, I will fear no evil: for thou art with me; thy rod and thy staff they comfort me."

One night, when I was a boy, I began bawling uncontrollably over the realization that I would die someday. Mom came and comforted me, telling me death was nothing to fear.

She told me so again in her final days, not in so many words, but in the way she faced death head-on. She was not eager to die — a woman who loved life so much could only say goodbye to it with great sadness. But having lived 88 good years, she was ready for the end.

There are worse things than death, she often said. She never was afraid to take controversial political stands. She refused to draw the blinds one night after she got a threatening phone call. They can only kill you once, she said; if you live in fear, you're letting them do it slowly.

"Thou preparest a table before me in the presence of mine enemies: thou annointest my head with oil; my cup runneth over."

Mom took a lot of heat over the years for being outspoken. Some men just don't appreciate a 4-foot-10-inch woman who speaks her mind.

But she never lost her love for people, even her adversaries. She'd always chat up waitresses: Where do you live? Oh, I know someone from there! Any kids? How old? (Please, Mom, can't we just order?)

Her cup overflowed with kindness. She was tough but ever remained Betty Jean, who loved music and children and laughter; who turned Keith Honey's head in high school, and remained his girl for the rest of her life.

"Surely goodness and mercy shall follow me all the days of my life: and I will dwell in the house of the Lord forever."

We all lose our parents, unless we go first. When it's your mother, it feels like you've been pulled from the earth.

All the old songs, psalms and prayers make a new kind of sense. They bring some comfort to your sorrow, like a mother at your bedside. As do all the loved ones who gather like angels.

Today, we celebrate mom's life at church. But her goodness will follow us all our days.

Aug. 6, 2011

Good game, Keith Honey, good game

Come back, Dad. I'm not ready to let you go.

I know you were ready to go for some time, ever since Mom went. I'd say life lost its thrill for you the moment she slipped away in her sleep that Sunday morning six months ago. You had been with her for more than 70 years. You had done everything else you set out to do and done it well. What was the point?

But we three needed you — my sister, brother and I. We needed you more than ever, without Mom there to guide us and nag us and laugh like a delighted child.

And so you stayed, for us. The ball game was over as far as you were concerned, but we needed you to keep playing.

I needed you to keep talking to me about good books and your life's adventures and baseball. It had been a long time since we could play catch like we used to in the side yard, when you taught me the curveball, coached me and watched me strike guys out with that big bender.

But we could still talk baseball, remember the delectable smell of Lakeland in spring and the pop of the gloves as the Tigers warmed up. We sat there, you and I, on a Friday evening as the game was about to begin, and life was as perfect as it could possibly be.

Although it's hard to get as perfect as it was back in Grand Rapids, when you tossed the Frisbee back and forth with us in the driveway, played Ping-Pong with us in the basement and wrestled all three of us at once on the living-room floor.

Perfect in their way were those midwinter Friday nights, me in my early teens, driving up U.S. 127 through the tunnel of snow, stopping in Clare for the most delicious meals I've ever eaten, burger and fries and a Coke in a little diner damp with snow melting off everyone's jeans.

Then, deep into the forest, trudging through the deep snow into the woodland retreat, opening the door and feeling the coldest cold ever. Turning on the lights. Climbing into the well pit to turn on the water. Stoking the wood stove and standing there as you unpacked, my back to the flames, my front still shivering.

You were not a perfect man, Dad, no one is; but in love and fatherhood, you aced it.

You encouraged us, always. You picked up the phone and always welcomed our voices with such good cheer. "Well Charles H!" You made us feel special, precious, loved through and through.

And all through the years, from the summer you went out West to fight fires, to flying through shrapnel over the South Pacific, to starting your family in a Memphis chicken coop, to building your career until you found your place in the sun teaching at MSU — you loved Mom.

You danced with her on New Year's Eve in Grandma and Grandpa's basement. You took long trips with her, to California, Alaska, Quebec. You sat and listened to her expound her strong opinions over a glass of wine, patiently letting her have the floor, always.

After all, she was your dark-haired beauty, the catch of McKenzie High. Always.

You'd almost drowned in the war, taken savage hits in hockey and football, felt your nerves fry through interminable meetings at work. But when Mom went, it was just too much.

Yeah, you took it with grace. You showed us kids how to grieve with dignity. But man, did you grieve. The love of your life, the candle in your window, she was gone.

From then on, it was just a matter of time for you.

We had one last summer and autumn with you, talking over so many things. You read good books and took solitary walks with your walker. You basked in the sun at Clark Home on Keller Lake, looked out at the ducks and Canada geese under a canopy of brilliant leaves.

I still see your beautiful, noble face, eyes closed, drinking in the life-giving sun like a wise Indian.

We watched the Tigers one more time. They didn't make the Series, but they beat the damn Yankees.

We had one more Thanksgiving, one more Christmas, one more New Year's together. You kept saying, "I'll make it to 90, and then we'll see." And that's just what you did.

Finally, your body said, enough. You've lived a glorious, full life, Keith Honey, but the light of your life has gone out. You miss her so. It's time.

You kept fighting to stay in the game, for us, but suddenly it just got to be too hard to live. First it was this, then it was that, and finally there were too many for you. Even such a strong, incredibly youthful man can only do so much.

And so, having pitched a near-perfect game, you finally came out. The manager walked slowly to the mound, while the hushed crowd watched. You handed him the ball and walked off the diamond. Everyone cried and cheered. You tipped your cap, a gentleman to the end, took one last look at the sky, then disappeared into the dugout.

You walked straight out of the ballpark into the field beyond, where Mom awaited you with open arms.

Jan. 21, 2012

Post-game wrap-up

Longtime Tigers broadcasters Mario Impemba and Rod Allen huddle to assess "Faith on First," its author and his contribution to baseball-themed literature.

Mario: Well Rod, Charles Honey went the full nine tonight, and for a rookie it wasn't a bad first outing.

Rod: Absolutely. He was a little shaky early on but as he settled in he started to find his rhythm. He showed good command and featured three or four really nice pitches, especially that curve ball that just dropped off the table at times. He's a work in progress but I think the team can look for good things from this youngster down the road.

Mario: I heard some of the guys in the clubhouse earlier saying that finding a focus will be a challenge for him. He tends to get distracted easily by side issues and that throws his mechanics off. So while he's got good stuff you really have to stay in that zone as a major league pitcher.

Rod: Absolutely. I think it's also going to be important for Charles to stick with his game plan and not let the opposition intimidate him. I mean let's face it, these are big-league hitters and they're going to look for your weaknesses. He needs to not back down when the big bats come up, stay within himself and pitch to his spots. Play his game, not theirs.

Mario: OK. Let's go now to a couple guys who knew Charles back in the day and are legends in their own right. Ernie Harwell and George Kell, nice to see you two back in the broadcast booth!

Ernie: Well it's great to be here, Mario. I can still hear the voice of the turtle way up here in heaven. And yes, I'd say that was a pretty nice first outing for the young man from Grand Rapids. As you say he's got some mechanics to work on, but he showed me a lot of poise for a rookie. He mixed his pitches and he came at the hitters. He didn't just stand there like a house by the side of the road.

George: Well that's right, Ernie. This young man has a lot of promise, even though he's actually not all that young. And Mario and Rod, you guys are too young to remember this, but Charles came up in baseball about the same time Ernie and I came on board with the Tigers. In fact, I remember the very game that made him a lifelong fan. I'll bet you do too, Ernie.

Ernie: I certainly do, George. It was Labor Day weekend of that magical season of 1961, when Mantle and Maris were chasing Babe Ruth's home run record and the Tigers were chasing the Yankees all season long. The Detroits came into that weekend just a game and a half behind the Bronx Bombers. On Friday night Don Mossi squared off against Whitey Ford and matched him for eight shutout innings. While the junior circuit's biggest crowd of the year watched the pitching duel at Yankee Stadium, Charles and his father were on his grandmother's front porch in Detroit listening to us broadcast the game. The Yanks pulled it out in the bottom of the ninth to go two and a half games up, and of course went on to win the AL pennant. Young Charles was impressed that someone could pitch as well as Mr. Mossi pitched that night and still lose. From that moment on, he was hooked on the great game of baseball, and the rest of course is history.

Mario: That's a great story, told as only the great Ernie Harwell can tell it. Anything you two would like to add before we sign off?

Ernie: I'd just like to say I know Charles to be a man of great faith, even though he may not always show it on the mound. He gets it pretty wrong sometimes, but he always gives 110 percent and never stops trying to understand the ways of heaven and earth. I look forward to meeting him at the pearly gates when he's ready to hang up his spikes.

George: And I'll be there right with you, Ernie. Maybe I'll bring a bat and we can have ourselves a game of pepper. (laughter)

Mario: Now that's something I'd like to see. Hey thank you guys for coming down to talk with us for a few minutes. I know the fans back home have really enjoyed seeing you again.

Rod: And say hi to the Babe and Sparky for us, ok?

Ernie: We certainly will, Rod. Just saw them yesterday at lunch, and they look great.

Just one more thing

I am sitting by the fire on a Sunday morning. Outside, the snows of early February are piled high, burying the yards and streets as they have these past two months. It is quiet and peaceful, my favorite time of day.

Like most people, I have always loved to sit by fires. When I was a boy we sat by a campfire at a point between Elk Lake and Round Lake, where we often spent summer vacation. We sang "Michael Row the Boat Ashore" and "She'll Be Comin' 'Round the Mountain" and told scary stories in the magical darkness.

Later, I hugged the fire through long evenings at our family's log cabin on the Muskegon River, near Falmouth in Missaukee County. It was a Franklin stove that drove away the biting cold of deep winter, a perimeter of warmth in which I read Marvel comics and Tolkien next to a lamp made of birch branches, then drowsed over the hypnotic glowing embers before crawling into my sleeping bag.

This fire by which I now sit is in a less rugged setting – a Kentwood subdivision – but it is no less enticing. It is the fireplace of my dear Andrea, a person I did not know six years ago but who has become the glowing hearth of my life.

Thus my life continues its winding course, like the swiftly running Muskegon of younger days. I canoed that river more than once with Brad, soul mate of my boyhood. We once plunged into its surprisingly cold water as we tried to navigate a tricky bend.

It was an unexpected adventure, like the night we lay in the cabin's loft listening to the Beatles' White Album till all hours, then took a long walk through the woods. We were startled by a bull in a farmer's meadow and I cut my leg jumping over the barbed wire.

You really don't want an adventure, Dad used to say with a chuckle. It means you've got trouble. I agree. I've always preferred the settled, predictable life. But that's not the life I've had. It has been an adventure, often stimulating, other times dramatic, always interesting.

Recent years have leaned heavily on the drama. A painful divorce, the implosion of the newspaper industry and the deaths of my parents left me standing in an entirely different landscape, in many respects starting over on a life that had seemed pretty well set. It's been a rugged lesson in the Buddhist concept of impermanence and Jesus' teaching to let tomorrow worry about itself.

Life as a freelance writer and teacher has been an adventure all right, and a rewarding one. But it sure hasn't been the peaceful picture I expected would one day paint itself. Instead of Paul McCartney's sentimental portrait of a couple contentedly sitting by the fireside, it's been a bumpy ride of reinvention.

And all God's people said, "Join the club."

Yet here I do sit by the fireside, in the cozy home of a lovely woman who leans heavily on Buddhism and loves the Beatles as much as I do. She was nowhere in sight when the swift-running course of my life took an unexpected turning. But when she appeared it was as if by design, waiting to take my hand to walk through this rugged new landscape.

A river has always run through my life – the Red Cedar in my boyhood home of Williamston, the Muskegon on those memorable cabin weekends, the Grand in my adult home of Grand Rapids. A fire has always fed my dreams along the way, huddled up on the riverbank as the stars came out overhead.

As I gaze at the fire now, it is not with the certainty that this was all planned out by God. But it is with the acceptance that this is how it had to be, and that it is not at all a bad way to be. It is a life filled with blessings, from precious family and worthy work to dear friends and my beloved Andrea.

And it is with a heart full of gratitude that I look into the flames and look back on the winding course of my life. I am grateful for the places it's taken me, and for the places I have yet to go.

Feb. 9, 2014

About the Author

Charles Honey is a freelance writer living in Grand Rapids, Michigan.

He writes a weekly religion column for The Grand Rapids Press/MLive.com, and is a staff writer for School News Network, an online news site of Kent Intermediate School District at www.schoolnewsnetwork.org.

He writes a blog on the spirituality of daily life at www.soulmailing.com. He also has taught college courses on journalism, the life journey and the spirituality of the Beatles.

To order copies of this book, or request a speaking engagement, you can reach him at honeycharlesm@gmail.com.